Ghost and Shamanic Tales of
True Hauntings

D1253554

y Comerford

Schiffer Publishing Ltd

4880 Lower Valley Road • Atglen, PA 19310

Cover image by Karen Ouellette
Back cover image of team by Fred Hobbs

DISCLAIMER: To protect the privacy of our clients, we have changed their names and locations. However, all events described are real.

Schiffer Books are available at special discounts for bulk purchases for sales promotions or premiums. Special editions, including personalized covers, corporate imprints, and excerpts can be created in large quantities for special needs. For more information contact the publisher:

Published by Schiffer Publishing Ltd.
4880 Lower Valley Road
Atglen, PA 19310
Phone: (610) 593-1777; Fax: (610) 593-2002
E-mail: Info@schifferbooks.com

For the largest selection of fine reference books on this and related subjects, please visit our website at **www.schifferbooks.com**
We are always looking for people to write books on new and related subjects. If you have an idea for a book, please contact us at
proposals@schifferbooks.com

This book may be purchased from the publisher.
Please try your bookstore first.
You may write for a free catalog.

In Europe, Schiffer books are distributed by
Bushwood Books
6 Marksbury Ave.
Kew Gardens
Surrey TW9 4JF England
Phone: 44 (0) 20 8392 8585; Fax: 44 (0) 20 8392 9876
E-mail: info@bushwoodbooks.co.uk
Website: www.bushwoodbooks.co.uk

Designed by Stephanie Daugherty
Type set in Marigold/Zurich BT

ISBN: 978-0-7643-4128-1
Printed in The United States

There are more things in Heaven and Earth...
than are dreamt of in your philosophy.

~ William Shakespeare

Acknowledgments

ALTHOUGH THE ACT OF WRITING IS A SOLITARY VENTURE, this book, in particular, could not have been possible without the help, love, and friendship of a dedicated group of people who make up The Spirit Light Network. To Steve, Amy, Becky, Cate. Lisa, Michelle, Joy, David, and Joanne, you've made this incredible journey even more incredible and enjoyable.

To Maureen Wood, psychic extraordinaire, for being the best friend anyone could ever ask for.

A huge hug and kudos to my husband, Larry. As a non-believer in the paranormal, he has always supported my passion for the Other Side. He keeps me grounded and always gives me a safe place to land.

To my mother – Mamacita – in whose blood runs the spiritual abilities that she has unselfishly passed down to me. She is the best cheerleader in the world.

To David and Sandy Vickery, who never gave up hope that I'd get published, even when I did.

To Peter Hunt and John Lawler for the years of friendship, wise counsel, encouragement and an eager ear to hear all my crazy ghost stories.

To Dinah Roseberry, a wonderful, talented editor and writer. You've been a joy to work with as has everyone in Schiffer Publishing. Thank you all for making this writer's dream come true.

And a huge thank you to the guidance and love we have consistently received from the Other Side. We are honored to be able to do what we do and we are blessed to have you helping us.

Contents

Foreword

~ Maureen Wood

Medium for the New England Ghost Project
Co-author of a *Ghost a Day and Ghost Chronicles:
17 Tales of True Hauntings*

F OR THOSE WHO WALK IN THE PARANORMAL REALM, a surreal existence of both this world and the next is imminent. Most often the spirits encountered are loving and kind. But then, there are those that defy all logic—defying even the laws of nature. There is no love. No compassion. Just a desire to attach themselves to the living. They are pariahs of the spirit world. This is when the Spirit Light Network intervenes. Like tightrope artists, they bridge the gap between the veil, and with their varied abilities, they council and provide peace and guidance to not only the living, but the deceased as well.

As both a friend and a medium for the New England Ghost Project, I've had the pleasure to work with Bety, Steve, and their team on several occasions. The Spirit Light Network is comprised of a group of gifted individuals who truly care so much for humanity that they willingly harbor the weight of the paranormal world on their shoulders—avengers if you will, volunteering their time in defense of those who would otherwise have nowhere else to turn. Through their shamanistic and mediumistic abilities, and most importantly, love, they enter the abyss. With guidance and spirit, they manage to lessen the negativity, regain balance, and ultimately reclaim a sense of peace for the afflicted individual and their surroundings.

I, for one, have seen both Bety and Steve work their *magic*. And now, through this book, each of you will also have the opportunity to walk hand in hand, reliving each case, a front row yet 'safe' seat, while you too experience each adventure right alongside them. So sit down, get comfortable, and enjoy. . . You are in for a ride of your life!

~ Maureen Wood

Introduction

sha-man: *someone who endeavors to connect to the spirit of all things*

IT HAS ALWAYS STRUCK ME AS AMAZING how life has a way of getting you where you need to be, even if, at the time, you don't realize it. (Or if you insist on kicking and screaming every inch of this road towards the unknown).

A few years ago, I found myself at a crossroads. The life that I had envisioned for myself had disintegrated and I didn't know what to do or where to turn. Like many who have faced such crises in their lives, I went in countless directions before finally turning to spirituality to try and find the answer. I met many teachers and learned different healing techniques, honed my psychic abilities, and read so many books I could have opened up my own library. Yet something was still missing.

Then, purely by accident, I heard about a shaman who was doing extraordinary work with people. I had no clue what a shaman was or what one did, but I was intrigued, so I made an appointment. It was on a warm spring evening in May of 2005 that I met Steve Wilson. At first, I didn't know what to make of this tall, 6-foot, 2-inch giant of a man with his faded, wrinkled dark green chinos and T-shirt with the picture of a howling wolf on it. My first thought was, what have I gotten myself into? But my curiosity outweighed my wariness and I decided to see what this shamanism stuff was all about.

It's a decision I have never regretted.

I learned about energy that night. How it affects us both consciously and unconsciously. How we can move and change our energy. How we can move and change someone *else's* energy. By the time I'd left that night, my body was tingling like a fourth of July firecracker and I felt incredibly alive. I knew then I had to learn everything I could from Steve. Over the course of the next few weeks and months, Steve and I became friends. Every time I saw him, I peppered him with questions about energy, about how it works, how it can be so easily affected by others. As our friendship grew, I began to nag him (something I'm pretty good at) to begin teaching his style of shamanism, which encapsulates many different cultures' beliefs and rituals.

He finally relented under my determined onslaught and our shaman classes began. It grew from a few students to include up to twenty-five participants. It brought me into contact with a wonderful group of people who were also seeking answers to explain the circuitous path their own lives had taken. We learned about energy from the living. Along the way, we also learned how the dead can affect us on an energetic level.

At this time, TV was full of paranormal shows, all showing pretty much the same thing – a group of people wandering around haunted locations with a slew of scientific instruments trying to prove or disprove the existence of ghosts. We would discuss these programs in our classes and one question kept coming up. Once a place is found to be haunted, what happens to the ghost? After the investigators have packed up their equipment and left, why are the ghosts left behind? Why aren't they helped to get to the next level of existence?

This is how and why the Spirit Light Network was created. As we grew in wisdom about how energy works, we began to understand why spirits remain stuck. We don't know all the answers, nor pretend to. But one thing became clear. It all comes down to energy. If a human being died in a state of despair, fear, or anger, those are heavy emotions. Think about how you feel when you're depressed or sad. You feel heavy. Now think about those times when you've been in love, or have had something wonderful happen to you. You feel light. Translate that to a spirit. If they died in a state of unrest, they are weighed down with those heavy emotions. The fact that they no longer have a physical body to process those emotions complicates the matter as well. We've learned, as shamans, how to physically feel the energy of everything around us. We take on the energies of these stuck spirits and move it through us in a process called grounding. As we move these emotions, the spirit will begin to lighten as they unburden themselves. Using his position as an ordained Spiritualist Minister, Steve will say a prayer that helps them understand that they can now relinquish whatever it is they've been holding onto. If we've done our job right, the spirit now has a choice to remain in the darkness (what we call the "in-between" place), or move on to the next plane of existence, which is one of peace and love.

We've been accused of taking the place of a Higher Consciousness when we do this. I'd like to say at the onset that we do not, nor ever would, usurp the place of the Creator in anything we do. But just as we are given the gift of free will as living human beings, we also have free will after death. What we do is show the stuck spirit that they have a choice. It is then up to them whether they wish to remain in the in-between place, or move on.

Most move on.

Almost from the beginning, our services were in great demand. It seems the veil is getting thinner between our world and the next, and there are more people experiencing hauntings who need help understanding what's going on. There are also more spirits becoming stuck. Our group has expanded into Connecticut and Northern New England and we get calls from other paranormal groups wanting to learn to do what we do.

In the following set of stories, I will talk about some of our more interesting investigations. There's a reason we've become the "go-to" group for other paranormal groups who have come across the darker entities and don't know or don't want to deal with them. We've done a great deal of personal work to get to a level where we don't fear those darker entities. We respect their power and have seen firsthand the damage they can cause in a person's life. We don't engage in a contest of wills, nor do we believe in antagonizing or provoking. You "leak" your own personal energy when you do this which only strengthens them. It all comes down to energy and how to use that energy to accomplish what needs to be accomplished – helping the spirit go Home and allowing the living to grow stronger to preclude any further attacks or occurrences.

I've also included in these stories techniques that you can use in your everyday life to improve the quality of your own existence. I'll detail how to ground out unwanted energies, how to cut cords with people who may be draining your energies and more. Each chapter will provide a how-to, as well as hopefully entertain you and teach you how important knowing how energy works is.

After all, you don't want to become a ghost yourself, do you?

Meet the Team

Rev. Steve Wilson

An ordained Spiritualist Minister and a certified shaman, Steve has spent a lifetime experiencing the Other Side. Teacher, mentor, leader, counselor, medium and psychic, he brings to the group a rich understanding of how the world works energetically and was instrumental in bringing together the members of The Spirit Light Network who share the philosophy that each spirit has a right to be shown that they have choices, even in death.

Bety Comerford

I'm a third generation psychic, empath, and medium, carrying on a family tradition, started in Cuba by my grandparents, of helping the dead cross. Since childhood, I have seen and heard the dead, yet it wasn't until I began studying shamanism in 2005 with Steve Wilson that I came to understand and expand my gifts. Together with Steve, I formed the Spirit Light Network to answer the question posed by many. "With all these paranormal groups and ghost shows on TV, why isn't anyone helping them get Home?" Why not, indeed?

Rebecca Curtin

Becky is a nurse who has been seeing and hearing Spirit since a youngster. She is a powerful empath and medium and is our EVP Queen, having captured some of our more interesting and chilling EVPs (electronic voice phenomena). She also works the camera and you'll see some of her work in this book. When she's not investigating hauntings, she's busy raising four rambunctious children, all of whom have inherited her psychic gifts.

Amy Wilkins

Amy is a hospice nurse and Becky's older sister. Her work with the dying has added another dimension to the group. She has studied South American Shamanism, having visited Peru several times and worked with the shamans there. She shares the title of EVP Queen and her photos will also be appearing here. Amy is a strong empath and psychic and has a deep connection to the energies of the Earth. She's a mother of two, who already show gifts of second sight.

Lisa Yoshida

Lisa comes from the world of academia, having degrees in psychology and speech pathology. She is also a certified meditation facilitator and journey counselor, a method in which she gently guides the client to discover for themselves a stronger sense of self so they can overcome fear and despair in order to achieve balance and happiness in their lives. As an empath and intuitive, Lisa offers sharp insight to those living people who are experiencing hauntings, and her gentle approach has helped many to come to grips with what is happening in their homes and in their lives.

Joy Gaffney

(Connecticut Chapter)

As one of the original members of the Spirit Light Network, she is now the founder and lead investigator for our Connecticut Chapter. Appearing on radio and television and through public lectures, she brings the message of Life After Death and techniques of Spirit Releasement to the general public. Utilizing her gifts as an empath, psychic/medium, and shaman healer, she assists others to find peace and reconciliation with their loved ones on both the physical and spiritual planes.

David Wetherell

(Connecticut Chapter)

David is also one of the original members and is the team's expert in land clearings. His shamanic connection to the earth energies and his deep interest in indigenous cultures and their shamanic practices has enabled the network to increase its activities in the area of land clearings and land blessings.

Cate Samuels

(Northern New England Chapter)

Cate is a very gifted medium, empath, energy healer, and spiritual counselor. She is a trained shaman and has a deep affinity for the druidic aspects of our work. She is currently studying for a B.A. in Pastoral Counseling.

Michelle Johnson

(Northern New England Chapter)

Michelle is adept at using her psychic and empathic abilities in her work as an artist and as a tour guide in various historical locations throughout New England. She is particularly gifted in clairaudience, a valuable asset when trying to ascertain the names of those who are haunting a particular area.

Joanne Martel

(Northern New England Chapter)

Joanne brings empathic and psychic abilities to her work in trying to help those on the other side to gain peace and understanding in the afterlife. She is also a reiki practitioner and combines her healing abilities with her job as a nurse.

1

I Didn't Mean To Do It

I N A PEACEFUL BEDROOM COMMUNITY JUST OUTSIDE OF BOSTON, on a silent neighborhood street that looks like countless others throughout the towns and villages of Massachusetts, there once sat a house whose tasteful appearance belied the tragedy that, despite the passage of sixty years, still permeated its walls. To drive by, you could easily miss it. The two-story white stucco, columned home with a detached garage blended in well with the other houses that sat close by on tiny lots. But if you chanced to linger for a moment and look up the steep stone staircase, you began to feel something intangible about the home. Something you couldn't quite put a finger on; a sense that although at first glance the house appeared welcoming and inviting, the more you stood in its presence, the more you realized that your hair stood on end, your stomach was uncharacteristically clenched, and you were overwhelmed by a deep sense of sadness and loss.

Lindsey Bell, a successful artist who paints vividly colored abstract canvases, bought the house four years before, for reasons she could never quite explain. As a single woman with two cats, the house was too big and needed a lot of work. Logically, it made no sense for her to buy such a white elephant. But drawn in a way she could not resist, she went ahead with the purchase of the circa 1930s home, and set about refurbishing and decorating, until at last she'd created another piece of art.

Yet throughout her time there, Lindsey slowly came to realize she was not alone. Doors opening and closing, cold spots, the strong sense of being followed and observed never left her. Moments of sadness, despair and longing would unexpectedly overwhelm her before instantly disappearing. Then there was the guest bedroom on the second floor that her two cats refused to enter, no matter how hard she tried to entice them. She knew her house was haunted. But by whom? And why?

With the last renovation completed, Lindsey reluctantly came to the decision that it was time to move on. She'd reached a turning point in her life, and quite frankly, there was nothing more to be done with the house. So she decided to sell. Yet, she found herself facing a strange dilemma. Was it fair to saddle whoever bought her house with the spirits who lingered there? What if the new owners had children? Could they deal with those strange moments of dread and despair or listen to doors opening and closing on their own without explanation?

Conscience told her she had to try her best to remove the spirits. But with no experience on how to do that, she didn't know where to turn. As luck would have it, she heard about our organization through an acquaintance and quickly contacted us.

Feeling we were her best hope in assisting the spirits of her home to move on, Lindsey called Steve Wilson, our team's lead investigator and co-founder. Driven by her experiences in the home, she'd set out to discover all she could about the history of the house and its past inhabitants. She'd managed to pull together an amazing amount of documentation and as soon as Steve answered the phone, she launched into what she'd discovered.

We have a policy in our group that we don't like to know anything about a location before we investigate. Unlike the majority of paranormal groups who rely solely on scientific equipment to prove or disprove the existence of spirits, we approach our investigations from a different point of view. Each member of the team has had personal experience with the paranormal. Many of us grew up seeing or hearing ghosts. We don't need to prove their existence. However, we do need to discover why a haunting is taking place. We, therefore, use both scientific equipment and our abilities as psychics and empaths to dig through the layers of emotion, of both the living and the dead, to get to the core reason of why a spirit has chosen to remain. Each member of the team will get a piece of the puzzle. At the end of the evening, we will begin to put the pieces together and hopefully come to a conclusion as to what is going on.

In order to uphold the integrity of what we discover using these abilities, we refrain from getting any facts from the client other than the fact that they are experiencing something out of the ordinary. Yet Lindsey seemed to feel the need to talk so Steve patiently listened as she went through the story.

An Investigation

A meeting was arranged and it was on a cool, crisp April evening that we found ourselves driving towards Boston. That night, the team consisted of Steve, Amy Wilkins, Lisa Yoshida, David Wetherell, Joy Gaffney and me.

The moon shone full in the chilly night sky, giving the appearance of a late autumn evening rather than early spring. The neighborhood was quiet, neat and well kept, its trimmed lawns throwing off deep shadows from the moonlight. Driving up a long winding street, each member began to get inklings of a turbulent energy. Not knowing the particulars of an investigation doesn't mean we don't *feel* emotions before we arrive. Since Steve had been careful not to share the details Lindsey had given him over the phone, we had no idea why we were feeling what we were. But the closer we drew to Lindsey's home, the more disruptive and violent the emotions became. We were tapped in, whether we wanted to be or not.

My stomach was in knots and my heart raced with a combination of fear and fury.

And dread.

Palpable, overwhelming dread.

Lindsey was anxiously awaiting us and already had the front door open as we parked and piled out of the car. A tall, attractive, well-spoken blond, she ushered us into a foyer of hardwood floors and beautifully bold colored paintings that she had painted herself hanging on the walls. The first impression I received upon entering was a sense of warmth and hospitality. But it quickly became clear there was something else. An underlying feeling of disquiet. Of something not quite right just beneath the surface.

"I'm so grateful you could make it," she said as she led us off the foyer into her dining room. A large square room, it was painted a warm pumpkin hue that offset the large dark cherry wood dining table and more of her autumn-themed artwork on the walls. On the table, she had thoughtfully laid out dip, chips, vegetables, and our particular favorite, chocolate.

"I haven't told the team what you and I discussed on the phone," Steve replied. "I don't want to cloud whatever they get."

"Do you mind if we wander around and take pictures?" I asked as I adjusted my camera for the lower lighting inside the home.

"Please, do whatever you need to do."

Our routine rarely varies whenever we do an investigation. Steve is a certified spiritualist minister and Lisa has an extensive background in communication, therapeutic journeywork and psychology. They sit with the client and listen to their story. It gives the person an opportunity to voice concerns, fears, curiosity, or simply gain reassurance that they are not losing their minds. The rest of the team explores the location, taking pictures, temperature readings, and EVPs. As we walk around, we begin the process of psychically tuning into the energy and making contact with the spirit to ascertain what happened to keep them from moving on.

Through our training as shamans and healers, we never judge what we feel or experience. We've come to understand that there's always more to a haunting than meets the eye. Entering a location, we don't rely on our first psychic impressions as the reason a spirit may be stuck. This is why we don't like to know the history or the story behind the haunting or location. We don't want anything we might psychically receive to be clouded or compromised by previously known details. We rely on our psychic intuition, empathic abilities, and mediumship gifts to dig, many times through layers of walls and false clues, to arrive at the likely causes that have prevented a spirit from moving on.

We have a saying that has proven accurate in the majority of our investigations. Drama in life equals drama in death. If a human being was dramatic, secretive, angry or shy in life, they will likely be that way in death. And if they are hiding something, they will throw up false trails and smokescreens to prevent us from getting at the truth.

We ask three basic questions during every investigation.

1. What kind of life did the spirit have that has made them unable to move on?
2. What secrets, if any, are they hiding that are keeping them stuck?
3. And, more importantly, what role is the living playing in the haunting?

Leaving Steve and Lisa to answer any questions Lindsey may have, the rest of the team wandered back into the foyer. I immediately noticed we were being shadowed by Lindsey's two fluffy calico colored cats. They were keenly keeping an eye on us, and no matter where we went, they were intent on following. I took pictures while Amy had her recorder ready to begin conducting EVP sessions.

Painful Discoveries

David was ahead of the small group and as soon he entered the living room, he gave a loud gasp and grabbed his head.

"Jeez!" he muttered under his breath. "Anybody else feeling this?"

At first, we felt nothing. Then an energy began to encircle us. As it drew nearer to each of us, we felt an excruciating pain in the front of our foreheads.

"Ow!" I yelped. "What the heck is that?"

"I feel as though my head is exploding into a million pieces," David replied, his face creased in pain and discomfort.

The pain increased and soon we were all cradling our heads. "Either someone got hit over the head, or they were shot," Joy spoke up. At that moment, the energy surrounding us spiked in intensity.

"I think you're on to something," David replied. "Whoever this is reacted to what you just said."

"I'm going to do some EVP work," Amy announced. "Maybe we can capture something on the recorder."

With my head feeling as though it were literally coming apart in my hands, I snapped off a few pictures, then swiftly stepped away from the swirling energy. Retracing my steps, I walked back into the foyer and headed towards the kitchen. It was a long, rectangular-shaped room with white cabinets and a butcher block island that neatly separated the room in two. From the dining room that adjoined the kitchen, I could hear the quiet murmur of voices as Steve, Lisa, and Lindsey discussed the subject of life after death. For the moment I was alone. I leaned against the butcher block and closed my eyes to concentrate. Immediately, I began to get a sense of an escalating argument between a man and a woman. I heard angry words being flung between the couple, though I couldn't quite hear what was actually being said. The emotions, though, were unmistakable. I felt my stomach tighten as I tapped into the highly charged atmosphere.

"This definitely feels like the center of the haunting," Joy remarked as she came up behind me. "Here and the threshold between the kitchen and the dining room. There's so much anger and resentment. No matter where I go, I hear the sounds of arguing."

So she was hearing it, too. Good confirmation that we were on the same track. She glanced around the kitchen one last time before heading towards the dining room. Before she left, she looked over her shoulder at me. "Whew. If these two were married, it was definitely *not* a match made in Heaven."

No kidding, I thought as the bitterness and antagonism between the couple continued to bombard me. It was getting difficult to separate who these emotions were coming from. Were they coming from the man? The woman? Both? Obviously, something very traumatic had happened here. But what that was had yet to be revealed.

Then I walked to the far corner of the kitchen.

I dug out my recorder from my jeans pocket and turned it on. "EVP session in the kitchen with Bety...OHMIGOD."

I almost dropped my recorder as an unbearably sharp blow suddenly and unexpectedly hit me in my stomach. I instantly buckled against the counter. The cats, which had been following me, quickly scampered out of the room, abandoning me to whatever force had just assaulted me.

I couldn't catch my breath. My stomach felt as though it were being ripped to shreds. Startled by the sudden onslaught of indescribable pain, I looked down to my abdomen and gasped. A psychic impression of blood was slowly spreading out all over my mint green sweater. Except I wasn't seeing my mint green sweater. I was seeing a white apron tied over an old-fashioned print dress. And I suddenly felt heavier, shorter as if I were morphing into someone else. I quickly realized I was going through a phenomenon called overshadowing – literally stepping into the energy of a spirit at the moment they are experiencing a particularly traumatic event and actually becoming them, reliving the moment as they lived it. It isn't a full possession. I'm still conscious and still aware of my surroundings. But for that moment, the lines blur and you are one with the spirit. I'd only gone through overshadowing once before. It's both fascinating and unnerving. This, however, was powerful, stronger than anything I'd ever felt before. I sat in its energy, enthralled and appalled at what I was going through.

I couldn't regain my feet as I lay slumped against the counter, the psychic blood stain growing ever wider across my stomach. I was now feeling shock and nausea and I could literally feel my life slowly slipping away from me.

My God, I thought to myself. I'm dying.

Back in the living room, Amy was tapping into the energies of an angry, dominant male.

"He's an extremely jealous person," she announced as she felt her heart burdened with the heaviness of suspicion and mistrust. "Doesn't want her looking at other men."

"Who? His wife?" Joy asked.

Amy closed her eyes. "Feels like it. They used to fight all the time about that. Actually, they used to fight about a lot of things. Yet, there's something else... I can't quite put my finger on it. He's blocking me somehow. It's as if he's hiding something." Her head suddenly jerked back. "What the --!" she exclaimed.

"What happened?" David asked.

Amy slowly brought her hand up to her cheek. "I think he just slapped me!"

David and Joy gathered around Amy and gasped when they saw a pink mark appear on her face.

"That was so weird," Amy murmured. "I can still feel where he made physical contact."

"You said he's hiding something," David surmised. "Then he hits you. Could it be you got too close to a secret he doesn't want revealed and tried to shut you up?"

As David was speaking, the room grew colder. Amy looked down at the temperature gauge in her hand and saw a ten-degree drop. "He certainly reacted to that."

David's eyes roamed the room. "We know you're hiding something," he said aloud. "It's just going to be a matter of time before we figure it out."

Once again, the trio felt an icy breeze envelop them. With the coldness came the unmistakable feeling of anger and rage.

"You're really ticking him off," Amy said.

"That's good. So, what do we have so far?"

"A husband and wife who fought all the time," Joy answered. "In the living room, we all felt tremendous head pain, obviously caused by some kind of trauma. And after what just happened, it's fair to say he could become violent when provoked. So, did this guy kill his wife?" She looked at Amy and David. "Or did she kill him?"

My nausea was increasing and I was beginning to feel faint. I knew I had to ground out this intensely uncomfortable energy or else I'd end up passed out on the floor.

Definitely not an option.

I closed my eyes and took a few deep breaths to center myself. It was time to use my shamanic training to move this energy out of me. Pushing past the physical discomfort, I began to slowly and methodically gather the pain and nausea that was centered in my stomach into a ball. I then gently pushed the ball down away from my mid-section, through my legs and shins and out the bottom of my feet, gatherifng loose tendrils of the energy into the ball as I moved it down. My feet soon began to tingle, indicating that the energy was moving out of me and into the ground. I repeated the exercise twice, each time feeling the pain and nausea lessen until it was completely gone. When I was done, I leaned back against the counter and wiped my forehead with the back of my hand.

Now, *that* had been interesting!

From the dining room, I heard Lisa's voice. "I keep hearing a man's voice say I didn't mean to do it. I didn't mean to hurt her."

With those words, a piece of the puzzle fell into place. I now had a general idea of what had occurred here. No sooner had I come to that conclusion than the hairs on the back of my neck suddenly stood up and a deep foreboding swirled in the pit of my stomach. A blast of frigid air blew across my cheek and shoulders and I shivered. No doors or windows were open and there had been no chill before Lisa spoke. I held my breath as I looked around the empty kitchen.

We were getting too close to the secrets in this house. And someone didn't like it.

I didn't have the temperature gauge with me, but I didn't need it to tell me the temperature was dropping. Fast. An energy, male in gender and fueled by rage, was building.

I normally don't allow a spirit to intimidate me. Giving into fear only makes a spirit stronger. But as the energy continued to build, I knew this was something I did not want to face alone. Before it could escalate out of control, I quickly left the room and joined the rest of the group who had gathered in the dining room.

"I want to take you all upstairs," Lindsey said. "I especially want you to see the room that the cats hate. Maybe you can tell me why they won't go in there, no matter what I do."

The energy was still with me, but its intensity lessened as the group followed Lindsey up the stairs. The cats followed while we entered the tastefully decorated master bedroom and the first guest bedroom, their huge yellow eyes silently studying us as we tried to pick up any psychic impressions. The guest bedroom offered nothing. In the master bedroom, Joy felt the energy of a woman looking in on Lindsey while she slept, which Lindsey readily confirmed.

An Imprint

The third bedroom, however, yielded another clue to the mystery of what had happened. As we moved towards it, we noticed the cats, who had been at our heels, refused to follow. They sat side by side at a distance, watching us, as if saying, "You're on your own in there."

"As you can see, the cats won't come in. And to tell you the truth, I don't like coming in here myself," Lindsey admitted as she stood near the doorway, her arms tightly crossed against her chest. "Before I called you in, someone suggested I try sageing the house. I did, but it didn't work." *Sageing* is a technique, originally used by Native Americans, to cleanse an area or person of negative energy. Burning white sage while saying a prayer is the common method employed.

"Sageing is only a temporary solution. It will make a spirit back away, but it won't release them," Steve explained. "After a while, they return because the energy that caused them to become stuck in the first place hasn't been released. You're then essentially back to square one."

We entered the sparsely decorated room. The team spread out on either side of the full-size bed and were instantly enveloped in deep grief and despair. And a shocked incomprehension. Unlike downstairs, however, there didn't appear to be anyone specifically attached to this energy. In the living room, we could easily identify the energy coming from a man, while in the kitchen it was definitely that of a woman. Yet in this small bedroom, the energy simply hung in the air, like a dense, suffocating fog.

Joy picks up the spirit of Irene.

"This feels like residual energy," Steve said. We all concurred.

"What's that?" Lindsey asked.

"It's an energy imprint. An event will occur that is so emotional in nature that it actually leaves an energetic imprint. Like a footprint, if you will. If you don't clear that energy out, it stays in place, playing itself over and over again. If there were an actual spirit up here, you would physically feel all their emotions and feelings. But we don't. All we're feeling is a memory of grief and sadness. As if someone were telling us about it without us actually feeling it."

"Why are the cats so afraid to come in here?" Lindsey asked.

"Because animals are extremely sensitive to energy. They're masters at reading it. And right now, there's a lot of dysfunctional energy stuck in this room and in this house," Steve replied. He then smiled. "Would you want to be in a room where a lot of yelling is taking place or where the energy is so heavy it feels as though you're being crushed under a heavy, wet blanket?"

Lindsey shook her head. "They scamper when they hear me raise my voice on the phone."

"There's your answer." He turned to us. "Have you finished walking through the house?" We nodded. "Then why don't we go back downstairs and see what the team has come up with?"

Gathering in the kitchen, I was careful to avoid the area where I'd experienced the overshadowing. Speaking first, I described the explosion in my stomach, the psychic impression of blood spreading over my abdomen and the extremely disquieting feeling of experiencing my life slipping away. "I believe the husband shot his wife while she was in the kitchen."

"So that explains why I kept hearing a man's voice saying he didn't mean to do it," Lisa said.

"Yet I don't get the sense she was the only one shot," David piped up. "When we went into the living room, I felt as though my head had been blown off. The energy surrounding that felt very male to me."

"I picked up on the fact that this man was extremely jealous of his wife and may have been physically abusive towards her," Amy pointed out. "Throughout this house, we've been hearing bits and pieces of a loud argument. In fact, lots of arguing. At first, we didn't know who shot who. But after hearing what Bety went through, it makes sense to say that after killing his wife in the kitchen, the man shot himself in or near the living room."

Lindsey gasped. "How did you--?" She whirled towards Steve. "Did you--?"

"I never said a thing. I told you they're pretty good. Now, why don't you tell them what happened?"

Lindsey looked at each of us, her eyes wide with amazement and a little fear. She took a moment to gather her thoughts, then slowly shared her story. "As you know, I've put this house on the market because it's just too big for me, even though when I first saw it, I had to have it. From the beginning, I kept feeling as though someone was watching me. Things would be moved and I'd hear doors opening and closing. One night, I came home late and found the light on in the attic and the attic door wide open. Thinking someone had broken in, I called the police. While I was waiting outside for them to arrive, a neighbor came over. Before I could say anything, she asked me if I was having trouble with the ghost. That was the first time I'd heard anyone mention the possibility of my home being haunted. So obviously the neighborhood knew something was going on in my house, though no one had any details. I tried to do some research, but came up with nothing. Then, within a week of putting the house on the market, a weird thing happened. A girlfriend told me she had met a woman who used to live in this house."

"Isn't that coincidental?" Steve replied knowingly.

"Exactly. I started emailing that previous owner and she told me that both she and her mother had also experienced the same things I was experiencing – the lights going on and off, the feeling of being watched. She told me she especially had a hard time at night. She would wake up screaming and point to the corner of her room where she kept seeing a dark shadow. What's interesting is that her room is the same room I sleep in and I've also awakened to see a dark shadow in the corner of the room. One of her last emails to me described a summer when she was about 14 years old. She remembered a car driving back and forth in front of the house. This went on for days. Finally, an elderly gentleman got out of the car and rang the doorbell. Turns out he used to live in this house and he told her and her mother that there had been a murder/suicide that took place in the house back in 1947. The murderer had been his father-in-law, a man named Clarence Sandie, and he had shot his wife in the stomach before putting the rifle in his mouth and shooting his head off."

As the name of Clarence Sandie echoed in the room, the temperature abruptly dropped again. The volatile energy I had felt earlier began to build once more, swirling in and among us.

"Do you feel that?" Steve asked. We all nodded. "He's angry that we know his name."

"Maybe I should stop," Lindsey replied, her frightened gaze darting back and forth in nervous agitation.

"The more he vents his anger, the more he weakens himself. Don't be afraid. Just go on with your story."

Some Answers

She took a deep breath, then continued. "Now that I had a name, I was able to find the newspaper article at the library that talked about what happened. Clarence was a twenty-year veteran of the fire department and was very respected, both at the station where he worked and about town. His wife's name was Irene and this was his second marriage. Apparently, on the morning of the shooting, at approximately 7 a.m., their daughter Sally, who was still in bed, heard Clarence tell Irene to call the fire department and tell them he wasn't going in because he wasn't feeling well. Irene did so and they both went downstairs where Irene started getting breakfast ready. Sally drifted off to sleep, only to be awakened a few moments later by the sounds of gunshots. When she rushed downstairs, she found her mother crumpled up in the corner of the kitchen with a gunshot wound to the stomach. In fact, Bety, it's in the same spot where you experienced her death. Clarence was lying between the kitchen and dining room with massive injuries to his head. The newspaper said the police surmised that after killing his wife, he'd put the barrel of a double barreled shotgun into his mouth and pulled the trigger. The rifle was lying near him." Lindsey looked up at us. "To add to Sally's horror, it was her nineteenth birthday."

The doorway where Clarence's body was found.

"By chance, is Sally's bedroom the one the cats won't go into?" I asked. Lindsey nodded. "Is Sally still alive?"

"As far as I could find out, she's in her 80s now and living on Martha's Vineyard."

"That's why it feels like residual energy up there," I concluded. "The heavy imprint of the shock and horror of finding her mother shot and her father's suicide would definitely stay rooted in her room."

As the tragic story unfolded, Clarence's energy continued to spike in fits of anger and rage. It surrounded us, and at times, pushed up against us in an effort to intimidate the group.

"He doesn't like us talking around him as if he's not here," Steve said.

"Okay. Maybe I really should stop now," Lindsey whispered.

"No. The more he reacts to us, the more he loses the energy of those emotions he's been carrying around all these years. That's good. It will be easier to help him when he's in a calmer state of mind."

"So basically you're not reacting to him. You're just letting him vent?" Lindsey asked.

"Exactly. If we were to react, he'd feed off that energy and get stronger, which would only escalate what we're experiencing already. That's why, whenever we do an investigation, we don't judge or react to what's there. The dead can't get any more energy from themselves;

they can only get it from the living. What are we doing if we or anyone reacts in fear or judgment or anger or intimidation? We're feeding the spirit what it needs and wants, which is our energy."

She thought about it for a moment. "That makes perfect sense," she admitted.

"I've got an idea." Steve said. "David, you, and I will stand on one side of the island. I want the ladies to stand on the other side."

We did as Steve asked, wondering what he was up to. When we were all in place, he crossed his arms across his chest and absently pulled on his goatee as he tried to pull all the pieces together.

"Okay. Clarence was an upstanding citizen. Well respected, a fireman. People liked him. By the way he's reacting as we uncover his secrets, his reputation was obviously very important to him. What puzzles me though is why would he shoot his wife at 7 a.m. in the morning? That's a strange time to shoot someone."

"I really think it was accidental," Lisa replied. "I kept hearing him say he didn't mean to do it."

"But why did he do it? What drives a good, decent man to shoot his wife in the stomach? Especially when, according to the newspaper, she did what he asked and phoned the fire department to tell them he wouldn't be coming in? And while she was in the middle of making breakfast for him?"

I suddenly felt my back turn ice cold. Goosebumps flew up and down my spine and the hair stood up on the back of my neck.

He wasn't very nice to me.

I caught my breath.

He put on different faces.

I was hearing Irene's voice in my head.

"Uh, guys," I replied slowly. "Irene is here."

Perhaps because I'd experienced the intimate moment of her death, Irene had attached herself to me and was now crowding my head with thoughts and emotions. I repeated her words, trying to pick through the rush of words from a woman who, sixty-two years after her death, had found her voice again.

"No offense, but some women know what buttons to push in men to get a reaction," Steve responded. "Maybe Clarence liked to look at other women and Irene caught him and gave him heck. We've already gathered that they argued a lot."

My back grew colder and a whoosh of anger swept through me. "She's upset because you think it's her fault for what happened here. She's saying he wasn't what you think he was." I felt a flash of pain on my cheek just as Amy had earlier. "He used to hit her."

"To shut her up because she didn't know when to stop nagging?"

It happened so fast, no one was prepared.

My body hurled itself across the butcher block island towards Steve.

"I'm going to pop you!" I screamed, my fist raised in the air in a murderous attempt to smash his face.

Somewhere behind me I heard the cats yowl in fear. Hands grabbed onto my sweater and yanked me back.

"Bety, she got into you!" Amy's voice filtered in as though from a great distance. "Push her out!"

As quickly as it happened, it was over. Irene's energy lifted off me, leaving me shaken and a bit embarrassed.

"Next time, let me know when you're going to piss her off, huh?" I said half-jokingly.

"I'm sorry about all this," Steve apologized. "Just testing a theory I had. It's pretty obvious Clarence and Irene are still stuck in their drama, reliving their arguments over and over. This just confirmed it."

"So what do you think happened the morning Clarence shot her?" Joy asked.

"There's something deeper going on here. I keep getting the sense that it has something to do with the first marriage."

Once again I felt Irene come up behind me. What she told me left me cold. I didn't want to repeat what I'd heard, but if we were going to solve this mystery, I had no choice.

"Irene is telling me there was a rape."

A powerful surge of anger flew through the room and we found ourselves clenching our chests in pain. "We're getting close to something because he's reacting to us," Steve said.

"When I did the research, I tried to figure out the dates of when things took place," Lindsey replied. "If I'm right, Clarence got a divorce in the 1920s."

"That's interesting," I said, falling back in my role as the team's historian. "Divorce wasn't that prevalent in the 20s among the average population. There was still a stigma about it."

"To put this all in perspective, let's say Irene discovered something about Clarence. Maybe there was a rape, maybe there wasn't. What matters is that he and Irene argued about it that morning and the gun went off," Steve said.

"Which would explain why Clarence gets so upset every time we dig a little deeper," Joy murmured.

"Especially when you consider how much his reputation meant to him," David added.

"According to the daughter," Lindsey spoke up, "her father was in the habit of cleaning his shotgun in the mornings. Maybe he was cleaning it, they got into their argument and it went off. When he realized what he had done, he was overcome with remorse and killed himself."

Raising Vibrations

The energy abruptly changed. The anger disappeared, replaced by a deep sense of guilt and sadness. It affected all of us and we remained silent as we took it in.

"Oh my," Lindsey finally spoke as she put her hand on her chest. "I can feel it so deeply in my heart. It makes me want to cry."

"That's good. By feeling Clarence's guilt, you're helping to move and release his energy. Let's do a prayer circle and see if we can get more of this energy moving."

Energy is composed of different levels of vibration. For example, if a person is depressed, their energy is at a low vibration. When a person is happy, their vibration is high. Using Steve's talents both as a spiritualist minister and shaman, we use a prayer circle to raise our own individual vibrational energy. We then combine those raised vibrations in order to help the spirits physically release whatever emotions they are still holding onto by allowing those emotions to move through us. It's the same as using a close friend to unburden yourself with. Rather than using words to help a spirit unburden themselves, we do it energetically and with our own bodies. A spirit no longer has a physical body to move emotions, but we do. As the emotions move through us, the spirit becomes lighter. No longer weighed down, they are able to move towards the Light.

We formed a circle and held hands. We closed our eyes and soon heard Steve intoning a sacred prayer.

Creator, we stand before You, hearts open, grounded to the earth that You created for us to walk upon. Many years ago an accident happened here, two souls jockeying for position to be right. But no one can be always right and no one can be always wrong. It is balance that is needed. Man is meant to walk in light as illuminator. Woman is meant to walk in light and also be illuminator. When each comes into position with each other, heaven is created on earth. This did not happen in this particular life. Each had an ideal on how they should be treated, how they should be loved, how they should be protected, and how they should be taken care of. The man we speak of had a belief he did something heinous that if allowed to come out in the world would destroy his very soul. The woman did not believe she was nurtured by the man she loved. Her heart was not loved the way it needed to be loved. And so there was accident, death, tragedy. We do not judge you. We do not hold you in sin or contempt. You were two souls, two living beings, doing that which you believed to be right and whether it was right or wrong, the only knowing that can be in your hearts is the knowing that the door is open for each of you. As you can see, there are other relatives, loved ones, friends standing in the doorway with outstretched hands, not to block you, but to bid you to come home. Suffer no more. Know the love your Creator holds for you is bigger than any sin you may have committed. This place is now cleared. The memory of what happened no longer resides here. Choose to leave, or choose to come with us as we leave so you can see the new world that does not hold you in contempt, but a world that loves you, a world that needs you to remember the love that you are; beings of open hearts that connect you to your God. That is what is required of you. Amen.

The room grew silent as our bodies hummed with raised vibrations. Emotions washed through us, feelings of guilt, anger, remorse, and contempt disappearing as Clarence and Irene began to realize the tragic end their lives and expectations of each other had led them to. As we took on their heavy emotions and ground it out, we in turn offered them love and forgiveness.

Unencumbered by the dense energies they'd been trapped in since 1947, Clarence and Irene became lighter. The doorway that would take them to the next part of their journey opened and we felt Clarence go through. As Irene approached, she hesitated. I had a sense of her looking back at Lindsey for a long moment, and I felt compassion flow from Irene to Lindsey. Then she was gone. Lindsey took a deep breath and let it out slowly.

"My God, that was so emotional," she said, her eyes brimming with tears.

"How does the house feel to you?"

She walked through the kitchen, dining room and living room. "It feels clear. I don't feel that heaviness anymore."

We joined her as she explored the upstairs and we smiled when we saw her cats enter the third bedroom and make themselves at home on the bed.

We gathered back in the dining room and sat down to eat the munchies Lindsey had provided. Investigations always make us hungry and we eagerly dove into the chips, pretzels, and M&Ms.

"You know, there were so many similarities between what happened here and my own life," Lindsey said in a thoughtful voice. "I have a set of grandparents who committed suicide. My mother found them." She jerked her head up as a thought occurred to her. "Oh my God! I just realized Mom was nineteen when all that happened. Just like Sally. Huh, imagine that." She shook her head. "Irene died when she was 41. When I was 41, I finally started finding my own voice. I started standing up for myself."

"Which is why she admired you," Steve pointed out. "You lived the life she didn't get to live. She was living through you. But living through someone else is living with half her power. Now that she's on the other side, she can come back someday and live her next life in her full power. She'll find her own strength, just as you did." Steve leaned over, warming to the subject. "We have found through many of our investigations that some people are drawn to certain houses because they're meant to help the spirits that are there. Think about it. You were drawn to this house because of the many parallels between your life and Irene's. It was no accident you came to live here."

"There were times I really felt that she was trying to help me, especially in those moments when I felt so depressed or doubtful that I could get my life in order."

"Believe it or not, as you helped yourself, you helped her. We just needed to provide that extra nudge for Irene and Clarence to realize they didn't need to hold onto their drama anymore."

As Lindsey took this in, we gathered our belongings. "Don't forget, if you need anything, or if you have any questions, call us. We'll come back as many times as we need to. Good luck with everything."

"Thank you! I feel better already."

As we walked toward our vehicle, I glanced back over my shoulder at the white stucco house with the green columns. I no longer felt my stomach tighten or the hair stand up on the back of my neck. Instead, in the cool New England evening, the house felt warm and homey. And, like Clarence and Irene, finally at peace.

Follow-Up

Lindsey informed us that after our visit, she no longer felt the presence of Irene and Clarence. To her surprise, it made her sad. "The house feels empty without them," she admitted. A month later, she sold her home and promptly bought another that she "simply had to have." As soon as she moved in, she discovered the previous owner, a 96-year-old woman, had recently died in the house. Like Lindsey, she'd been a fiercely independent artist who had struggled between her life as an artist and her needs as a woman. Had Lindsey been led again to a house that needed her help? Only time would tell.

Grounding

Grounding is a technique where you literally ground out any emotions, whether yours or someone else's that adversely affect you and keep you from feeling your best. This is an especially important technique to learn if you are sensitive to other people's emotions or if you feel overwhelmed by crowds or heavy emotions. Close your eyes and imagine a round red ball about a foot beneath the soles of your feet. Focus your attention on this red ball. The more you focus on this ball, the more you should begin to feel your emotions slowly moving from your head, down through your chest and stomach, slowly cascading down your abdomen and legs and out the bottom of your feet into this ball. You may feel your feet tingling and you will begin to feel lighter the more you do this. Grounding really is that simple. The more you do this, the more you will train your body to automatically ground.

2

I Don't Want To Be Like You People

EVERYONE HAS HEARD OF HAUNTED HOUSES, haunted land, even haunted toys and household articles. However, in the course of our many years of investigations, we've stumbled upon another phenomenon that, as far as we know, isn't much talked about, but which is much more prevalent than we ever thought possible.

We're talking about haunted people.

This goes beyond those human beings who seem to be haunted by a particular entity that follows them from place to place. A haunted person is someone who unwittingly attracts a variety of spirits to themselves, often not understanding why or how to put a stop to it. The following investigation details the experiences of such a person. Despite her fierce resistance and absolute terror of the Other Side, she was and remains a haunted person.

Peeling Layers

"I don't want to be like you people. I don't want to be afraid of my own home. I want this all to go away and never come back."

Not the most auspicious beginning to an investigation.

It started with a phone call from my good friend, Karen Cunningham. A talented Tarot card reader, Karen was doing readings at a charity-sponsored psychic fair when she found herself doing a reading for someone whose problems went far beyond wondering if she was going to meet Mr. Right or if she was going to win the lottery.

"Her name is Janine Montgomery and she really needs your help. She bought a condo two months ago and after moving in, weird things started to happen. It's gotten so bad, she refuses to spend the night there. She's absolutely terrified of the place and has basically moved in with her sister. She goes back about twice a week to pick up a change of clothes."

Knowing our policy of not wanting to know any details about an upcoming investigation, Karen refrained from continuing the story.

Instead, she acted as go-between, helping to set up a meeting at Janine's condo for that weekend.

It was early November when we scheduled to meet Janine at her home. With Thanksgiving just two weeks away, the other team members were busy with family obligations. Steve and I opted to go to see what we could do. If warranted, we would get the other team members to pay a follow-up visit.

The evening's temperatures were in the low teens, with a hint of snow in the air. We drove alongside the ice-packed Merrimack River, past the sprawling campus of the University of Massachusetts, its cold streets empty of students. As we drew closer to the address Karen had provided, Steve and I began to feel a prickling of our senses. The sensations surprised us.

"Are you feeling that?" I asked as I slowed my car at the red light.

"Yeah. It's definitely not what I expected."

"Me neither. I mean, is this for real?"

I took my eyes off the road and looked over to Steve. His features mirrored mine. Just what was going on here?

It was almost 8 p.m. by the time we pulled into Janine's complex. There were three long, garden-style brick buildings standing side by side, the parking lot full on this chilly Saturday evening. I inwardly groaned as we passed parked car after parked car. I didn't relish walking any distance in this cold. But luck was with us. As we pulled up to Janine's building, there was an empty spot right outside the front door.

We grabbed camera, temperature gauge, and EMF meter and quickly dashed into the warm, carpeted foyer. I'd barely finished pressing the button before we were buzzed in.

A young woman of average height with brown shoulder-length curly hair stood on the second-floor landing waiting for us. She was dressed in a pair of black running pants and a white T-shirt, and her face was marked with anxiety.

"Thank you so much for coming," she greeted us with a polite wariness. It was a reaction we were becoming all too familiar with. She didn't want to hear how or why this was happening to her. She just wanted us to make it all disappear. She could then shut everything away – us, the ghosts, her fear, and have her life return to normal.

Unfortunately, it doesn't always work that way.

After quick introductions, we entered the condo. It was beautifully decorated in browns and deep reds and the lighted pillar candles exuded a pleasing, spicy aroma. Karen was waiting for us in the living room. Having brought us all together, she was eager to find the root cause of Janine's nocturnal visitors and insisted on being present.

Although we maintained a look of professionalism on our faces, both Steve and I exchanged perplexed looks. Now that we were actually standing in the condo, we found that our impressions in the car had not been wrong.

The little information we'd received from Karen led us to believe we would be dealing with a malevolent energy. After all, Janine was being prevented from living in her own home and I could tell by the look on her face that she hated being there now, despite the presence of three other people. However, instead of coming face to face with a negative spirit, or feeling the telltale pain in my chest that indicated the presence of a lower energy, we felt ourselves bombarded with love. And a sad, poignant loneliness.

Not everyone who dies remains stuck in what we call the in-between place. Many continue on their journey and cross over to a higher plane of existence. Once they've crossed over, they can and do return, perhaps to check on a loved one or to escort a dying relative to the Other Side. When we encounter these spirits, we can tell they've crossed because we feel pure love from their spirits. However, those that remain stuck are still holding onto earthly emotions – anger, sadness, guilt, etc. Such heavy emotions prevent their energetic vibration to rise enough to see the Light and move towards it. These entities are the ones responsible for many of the hauntings that occur worldwide.

What surprised Steve and I was the lack of anger or violence. Were we missing something? Were we being tricked by whatever was here?

Perhaps the entity was hiding in another room. Maybe it was concealing its violence behind a smoke screen of benign emotions. The only way to find out was to do a walkthrough of the two-bedroom condo and start peeling away the layers. Before we could ask permission to begin our walkthrough, Janine launched into her story. We wanted to stop her and get psychic impressions first, but she needed to give voice to her terror. We had no choice but to sit down on the couch and hear her out.

"Everything started a few days after I moved in. I'd be awakened in the middle of the night by the sounds of scratching on the wall behind my headboard. At first, I thought it might be the pipes, but I had them checked out. Several times, in fact. Of course the maintenance men never found anything. When I asked both my upstairs and downstairs neighbors if they heard any sounds, they thought I was crazy. Then, during the day, I started feeling a cold breeze blow across my left arm. No matter what room I went in, the cold breeze followed."

"Did this happen at a particular time of day?" Steve asked.

"Not really. It would start as soon as I got home from work and continue off and on until I went to bed at night. I checked everywhere to make sure there were no drafts, but this place is insulated pretty well. Then it started on my face. It would never last long. Just as quickly as it started, it would stop. On top of all that, I felt as though someone were constantly watching me. The only place I feel safe is in my bathroom." She gave us a lopsided smile. "At least whatever is here respects my privacy."

"Tell her about last week," Karen prompted.

Janine visibly shuddered at the memory. "I've been awakened several times by something shaking my bed and pulling on my covers. But just when I thought it couldn't get any worse—"

She stopped speaking, her eyes filling with tears. As she fought for composure, she dug her nails into the palms of her hands and forced herself to go on. "You have to understand, this is the first place I've ever owned. I really thought I was going to be happy here. But after weeks of sleeping at my sister's, I realized I couldn't keep imposing on her. I mean, how insane is it to be afraid of sleeping in your own house? So I made myself come back. It seemed like forever before I could fall asleep. It was around three in the morning and I was finally drifting off." She hesitated as she nervously eyed us. "You're going to think I'm crazy."

Steve laughed. "Believe me, Bety and I are the *last* people to think you're crazy."

Buoyed by our sincerity, she sighed and continued with her story. "As I said, I was just starting to fall asleep when I suddenly heard my accordion that I keep in the closet in the extra bedroom start to play. There's absolutely no explanation for it. I've lugged that accordion around with me for years and that's the first time I've ever heard it play by itself. It was a couple of notes, but it was definitely playing. That was the last straw. I grabbed whatever I could and drove to my sister's house. This is the first time I've been back." By the time she'd finished her tale, she was hugging herself tightly. It didn't take a psychic to see how upset and close to the edge she was by the occurrences in what was supposed to be her place of refuge.

Now that she'd finished her story, Janine seemed to curl up into herself. Steve took the opportunity to jump to his feet. "Do you mind if we walk around and see what we pick up?" he asked.

"Do whatever you need to do. Just get whatever is here out! Or else I'm selling this place."

She meant it. Sadly, the real estate market was beginning its downward spiral and Janine stood to lose a great deal of money if she tried to sell. Pressure to help her feel comfortable in her own home was mounting.

Doin' What We Do

Steve and I walked through her kitchen and bathroom, trying to sense anything that would want to hurt Janine. We jokingly call this using our "spider" sense. Just as a spider tests the air with the sensitive hairs on its long legs, we put out our psychic feelers and attempt to sense any changes of energy. Both Karen and I were snapping away on our digital cameras while Steve held both the temperature gauge and the EMF meter.

So far, we felt nothing threatening or disruptive. We were still enveloped in that bewildering sense of love. When we entered the master bedroom and approached the headboard, Steve and I came to an abrupt standstill. It was as if we'd walked into a giant refrigerator.

"The temperature gauge just dropped twenty degrees," Steve announced.

"I knew it! I knew there was something hanging out in my bedroom," Janine cried out.

Steve walked to the other side of the room furthest from the headboard. "It's reading a normal 75 degrees here."

"Of course. It's because my bed is over here and it likes to bother me at night," Janine said.

As Janine spoke, the energy moved away. When Steve returned to the headboard, the temperature gauge remained at 75. We checked for drafts, open windows, anything that would have made the gauge react the way it did. But we found nothing.

As we started to leave the bedroom, Steve slowed his step. At the same moment, I felt the unmistakable presence of not one spirit, but three moving around us. Two remained hazy to me; I couldn't quite make out what they looked like or who they were. The third however, seemed to take a shine to me. I could tell it was a male and he was soon standing next to me, my arms erupting in goosebumps to indicate his icy presence.

Steve and I said nothing to each other. We didn't want to alarm Janine yet. We still didn't know who these spirits were or why they'd staked themselves out in Janine's apartment.

As I turned to take a picture, Karen caught my eye. She silently mouthed to me that she too was feeling the presence of the spirits. I quietly nodded as the two of us continued to snap away, hoping to capture an image or anything that would collaborate what we were sensing.

By the time we reached the second bedroom where the incident with the accordion had occurred, Steve and I glanced at each other in concern. We still weren't feeling anything frightening. No violence, no anger. No menacing presence. Just love. And that love seemed to be coming from the three spirits who were keeping very close to us.

When I "see" a spirit, it appears as an image in my mind's eye. I see them the same way a person will see details of a daydream, or a dream at night. Many times, I can't make out specific facial features, but I will see their height, weight, hair, and the type of clothing they're wearing. Because of my degree in and love of history, I can usually pinpoint what time era they're from by the clothes they're wearing. I hear when they speak to me and I will feel whatever they're feeling at that moment.

Steve takes his abilities one step further. He does see faces and will accurately describe what the spirit looks like, right down to the shoes they're wearing or the cologne they have on.

Karen had recently begun honing her mediumship abilities and was able to sense the three spirits, though, like me, she could only make out a general description of what they looked like.

Janine used her second bedroom as a storage area. Packing boxes were still stacked up against the wall, silent testimony to her unwillingness to completely move into an apartment that was scaring her half to death.

I looked over to Steve and noticed how still he had become. Guessing that he was in the middle of a silent conversation with the spirits who had followed us into the bedroom, I turned my attention to the closet. I was anxious to see this accordion that had come to life. The door was open and I saw it resting against the far wall. I lifted my hand and was starting to reach for it when I suddenly felt a blast of cold air hit me in the face. I blinked my eyes in surprise and took a step back just as the EMF meter began to furiously beep.

"What happened?" Janine immediately asked. "Oh my God! Is there really a ghost in there? Is that why that thing is going off?"

I held my hand up. "Let's make sure it's not wiring in the walls. Sometimes that will trigger a response."

I felt the spirits move away from the meter as I scanned the walls both inside and out of the closet. The meter remained silent. However, Karen, who was standing closer to Steve, gave a little shudder.

"They're here," she remarked in perfect imitation of the little girl in the movie *Poltergeist*.

"*They*?" Janine shrieked. "You mean there's more than one in here?"

The Chill of Truth

I started snapping off pictures, only to abruptly stop when I became aware of cold air slowly licking against my arms and neck. I stood still, feeling the air pass along my right shoulder, trace a line along my back, my left shoulder, and around to my face. My skin erupted into tiny goosebumps a second time as I held my breath. In my mind's eye, I saw the fuzzy outline of the man who'd made contact with me in the master bedroom. He was becoming clearer and I could see he was dressed in leather chaps, while at the same time I heard the distinct sound of a motorcycle engine revving up.

"Are you feeling this, Steve?" I asked quietly.

"Not sure. I've got two entities I'm dealing with over here."

"*Two?*" Janine gasped.

"I think we should go back to the living room and compare notes," Steve suggested. We trooped back into the living room and made ourselves comfortable.

"I'm not sure I want to hear what you have to say," Janine admitted as she nervously clasped and unclasped her hands.

"It's not as bad as you think," Steve reassured her. "In fact, to be perfectly honest with you, I don't feel anything bad. And believe me,

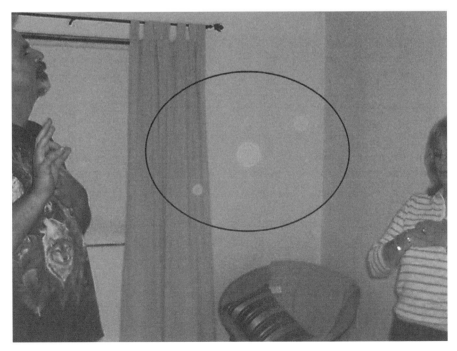

Steve and I saying a sacred prayer. Note the three orbs between us indicating the three spirits inhabiting Janine's condominium.

we would know it if there was something that was of a lower energy here. But ever since we arrived, all I've been feeling is love."

"Same here," I concurred.

"But why all the noise? Why the scratching on the wall, the pulling on my sheets, the damned accordion playing on its own?"

"Because they're trying to get your attention."

"Why?"

"Because whether you like it or not, you're a light."

She sighed in frustration. "What does that mean?"

Steve leaned forward and gave her a knowing look. "This isn't the first time you've had to deal with spirits, is it?"

Janine stared at him for a moment, then angrily looked away. We could feel her once again curling into herself. It was obvious Steve had touched a nerve, but rather than pursue it and upset Janine further, he changed tactics. "You've got three spirits here. One is a homeless man, the other is an elderly woman."

"And the third is a biker," I chimed in.

Janine sat back with a thud. "Three? My God, I'm living in a bus station!"

"I can see how maybe the woman and the biker might have lived in these condos at one time and decided to stick around, but why would a homeless man be here?" Karen asked.

"How old are these buildings?" I asked.

"About ten years old, I think," Janine answered.

"And before that?"

"Just a field."

I turned to Steve. "Do you think the homeless man died on the property before it was turned into condos?"

He shrugged. "It doesn't really matter where he died. The fact is that he's here now."

"But why?" Janine asked again. "What does he want?"

"Acknowledgment."

"Huh?"

"What does the average person do when they see a homeless person? They ignore them. Pretend they're not there. This man spent his whole life being ignored. As far as society was concerned, he was a nobody. He's come to you because he wants to be acknowledged. He wants someone to know that he lived. That he had a life. The old woman may not have been homeless, but she led a very lonely existence in the end. She was once beautiful, but as her beauty faded, she withdrew from life, trying desperately to recapture her youth. I can see her face, wrinkled and old with bright red lipstick on her mouth and heavy make-up on her eyes and cheeks."

"You can really see that?" Janine asked, the skepticism obvious in her voice.

"I've seen spirits all my life. I interact as easily with them as I do with you, or Bety, or Karen. The only difference between us is that they no longer have a physical body. Until they cross to the Other Side, they still feel as we feel. They hurt, they cry, they get angry. And in this case, they still feel the loneliness and sadness they felt in life."

"I still don't get why they're bothering me."

Steve took a deep breath. "Because you're a natural medium."

"I told you before. I'm not like you people. I don't *want* to be like you people."

I almost said "too late," but quickly realized flippancy was not going to help here. I held my tongue and watched as Janine lapsed into a moody silence. I could tell she didn't know what to think. Here she was, convinced that something was out to get her, while we were insisting there was nothing evil radiating from these spirits. We had no proof. It was just our word, backed up by the psychic images and impressions we were getting. My heart went out to Janine. I wasn't sure what else we could do to convince her that what we were getting was as true and real as it was ever going to get. All I could do was hope that we'd captured something on the camera or my voice recorder that would convince her we weren't crazy.

Sensing her mood, I debated whether to bring up the third spirit. But before I could decide whether I wanted to pile more distressing information on her, I felt the biker's energy swirl around me again, followed by that unmistakable sound of a motorcycle engine.

He obviously wanted to be heard. So I plunged ahead.

"Then there's the biker," I tentatively replied.

"Right," she muttered.

Images and words began bombarding me and I spoke quickly, trying to keep up with all the information he was throwing at me. "I don't know who he is," I said, "but he says you do. He's telling me to remind you that he always took care of you. He's still taking care of you." I closed my eyes to concentrate better. "I'm hearing the roar of a motorcycle." I suddenly felt an excruciating pain in my head and chest, knocking the breath right out of me. "I think he died in a motorcycle accident," I gasped. "I'd say chest and head trauma."

I let the energy of the accident move through me and when I could breathe again, I saw the image of him standing in front of me. "He's tall and thin, but tough," I described. "He was definitely someone you didn't mess with. Tattoos, too. I'm seeing tattoos all up and down his arms. And drinks. He's showing me a bar with shot glasses on it. But he's not drinking from the glasses. He's cleaning them."

The room grew silent.

I unconsciously held my breath as I waited for a reaction from Janine. Did she really know this spirit? Was he playing with me?

Did she believe Steve and I were insane?

"His name is Brian," Steve replied softly.

The reaction was immediate. Janine gave a start. Her eyes grew wide, her jaw dropped. "Oh my God," she whispered.

"He really cared about you," I continued. "He thought the world of you."

"I take it you know who he is," Steve said.

She slowly nodded. "I can't believe this. How did you—?"

Steve smiled. "He told us."

Janine glanced around the room as if expecting to see him.

"Tell us about him," Karen gently prodded.

Janine hesitated, then heaved a heavy sigh. "I left home when I was eighteen. I found a job working as a waitress in a biker bar. As you can imagine, the guys that came in there were pretty rough, but the tips were great, especially for a kid just out of high school. The bartender took a shine to me and always looked after me. Nobody dared mess with me when he was around. It was like having a big brother watching over me." She looked up to meet our eyes. "His name was Brian and he was just the way you described him."

Both Steve and I felt a chill run through our bodies. We consider this the chill of truth. When we hit upon a particular truth about a situation or a spirit, the vibrations line up, giving us a jolt of energy that gives us goosebumps. The more Janine reminisced about Brian, the lighter his energy became.

"Do you know how he died?" I asked, wondering if what I'd perceived as a motorcycle accident was accurate. She shook her head.

"We lost touch a long time ago. But it wouldn't surprise me if he died on his bike. He loved to race. I was always telling him that he drove too fast."

"He's here because he wants you to know that despite death, he's still looking after you."

"He doesn't need to do that anymore," Janine replied. She glanced up at the ceiling. "I'm okay, Brian. I appreciate you wanting to stay, but you don't have to anymore. As you can see, I'm fine. Really. You can move on."

"I'd like to say a little prayer," Steve said as he stood up and gathered us all into a circle. We held hands and listened as he began to speak, acknowledging the existence of the homeless man and the elderly woman. He thanked Brian for all he had done on Janine's behalf and gave him permission to relinquish that responsibility and move into the Light. As he spoke, I felt my vibration grow until my body hummed, my heart huge with unconditional love for these lost souls who had at one time walked upon this earth and taken part in all that makes us human. I felt their sadness, their loneliness wash through me, grounding it through my feet until my toes felt as though they were on fire.

Near the end of the prayer, I felt my body shudder as their energy detached and they moved into the Light. When we were done, we asked Janine to walk around the condo.

"It feels lighter already," she announced when she re-entered the living room.

"So do you think you can finally start living in your own place?" Karen asked.

She smiled confidently. "I think I can."

Follow-Up

Despite a successful conclusion to the evening, within a few months we were called back on three separate occasions. It seemed that Janine's condo was indeed becoming a bus station of the spiritual sort. Not only was she still hearing noises, but now she was feeling a set of small hands grabbing the bottom of her shirt whenever she walked throughout her home. Upon arriving at the condo, we were able to tell her that the small hands belonged to a young girl who had gone to Janine's day care center. She'd recently died of cancer, a death that Janine, who had been close to the girl, deeply mourned.

We successfully cleared the apartment on each visit, only to be confronted with a new set of spirits the next time we visited. We consistently offered to do a healing on Janine, not only to help her understand what was going on, but to get her back into a balanced energetic state, but she resisted.

After our fourth visit, she finally relented and allowed Steve to perform a healing on her. During the healing, she reluctantly admitted that Steve was right when he told her she'd been experiencing spirits all her life. Since her childhood, she'd seen and heard ghosts. It grew so disruptive that she deliberately closed herself off, determined not to have that as part of her life. She couldn't understand why she had this gift and her sister didn't since, as she said, "Bethany *wants* to see ghosts. I don't."

Unfortunately, it doesn't work that way. We came up with a term for a person like Janine. We call them "a haunted person." This is someone who is naturally psychic, but because of fear or lack of information, has tried to turn away from their gifts. But as Janine, and countless others like her have discovered, gifts such as this cannot be turned off forever.

Janine realized she couldn't deny her gifts any longer. She is a light and spirits who are lost, seek out that light. They were finding her wherever she went and followed her home. We taught her that these gifts are not something to be feared. Through her healing with Steve, he was able to assist her in working through her fears. In time, she came to accept that she was indeed a natural medium. We taught her how to stay out of fear and understand that the spirits that were coming to her were simply seeking help. By radiating love and acceptance and not falling into fear, she could help move their energy.

Energy is composed of different vibrational levels. It is our belief, gained through our investigations, that each human being comes to this life to learn certain lessons. As each lesson is learned, their energy vibration becomes higher. It is the same as removing a heavy stone from your pocket. With each lesson learned, the burden in your pocket becomes lighter. But what happens if a person has refused to learn any of their lessons? What if they've remained stuck in a dysfunctional energy pattern, such as anger or guilt? What if, like Brian, they've died with a heavy sense of responsibility for another human being that doesn't allow them to let go of this responsibility? Or, like the homeless man and the older lady, sad because they were forgotten? Because they no longer have a physical body, they cannot process these emotions. That's where we, and people like Janine, come in. By allowing ourselves not to judge them, but simply feeling and grounding their emotions for them, they are able to "lighten" up. The burdens are lifted and they are able to reach that energy threshold where they can see the Light. Then they can decide whether they want to move towards it. Once they feel the peace and love that radiates from the Other Side, they usually leave.

But not always…

A Simple Way to Balance Yourself

Start by placing your left hand over your heart and your right hand over your belly (your heart is considered the fourth chakra [chakras are energy points in our bodies that hold emotions] and your belly is your third chakra). Picture a band of white light moving in a circular motion between your heart and belly for a few moments. With practice, you'll start to feel the energy moving. Now move your left hand up to your throat (fifth chakra) and your right down to a spot below your belly button (second chakra). Expand the circular band of white light to now move from below your belly button, up to your throat, down through your heart and belly and back to the spot below your belly button, then up again. Do this for a few moments. Next, move your left hand up to the top of your head (your crown or seventh chakra) and move your right hand to a spot near where your legs meet your torso (the first chakra). Expand the circular band of energy to encompass all these chakras or energy points. Do this for a few moments. When you are done, place both your hands over your heart and say: "I am." This acknowledges the divine spark within you. You can balance yourself in the morning before you start your day or in the evening, especially if you've had a stressful day.

3

The British Are Coming

I T WAS A WARM JUNE EVENING, the type that promises summer is finally here. In New England, a region where winters seem to intermittently drag on, that's always a treat. Steve, Lisa, Amy, Becky, and I were on our way to visit a home in Arlington, Massachusetts, a sprawling suburb just outside Boston. This particular case had been referred to us by Kate Schluter, a psychotherapist who specializes in blending solid psychological principles with strong spirituality-based mind-body techniques. As the Founder of the Center for Transformational Healing, she is sometimes called upon to counsel a person whose issues stem from being sensitive to the Other Side.

Whenever a child is involved, we place it at the top of our list to investigate. In this instance, ten-year-old Nathan was awakening every night, screaming and unable to sleep. He would tell his mother "the bloody men" were back. He'd describe, in vivid detail, the men in rags, sometimes bloodied, sometimes crying with pain and anger, trooping through his bedroom. At first, his mother believed they were just nightmares. But as the incidences increased, and Nathan began showing signs of sleep deprivation and withdrawal, she took him to see Kate. Kate immediately recognized that more was going on than just a child experiencing night terrors. She called Amy, who had studied Peruvian shamanism under Kate, and asked if our group could take a look at this case. We quickly accepted.

After getting off the main boulevard that runs through Arlington, we found ourselves in a quiet neighborhood of well-kept houses and immaculate lawns. The house itself was a white ranch with a lovely picket fence outside, adorned with flowering rose bushes.

Kate, an attractive blonde with a warm, nurturing personality was waiting for us when we arrived. She was curious to see what we would find and asked to be present for the investigation.

We entered the house and met Nathan, a quiet boy with dark brown hair and soulful eyes, and his mother, Abby, a trim woman of medium height and shoulder-length ash blonde hair.

At first, Nathan was shy, sitting on the couch as close as he possibly could to his mother. His face was drawn and weary, which wasn't surprising under the circumstances. We introduced ourselves and Steve immediately set about creating a rapport between himself and the boy. In his private practice, Steve has counseled many children who have experienced ghosts and their parents who have no idea how to cope with the situation. He sat across from Nathan so they could be eye level with each other.

"How are you doing, Nathan?" he asked in a quiet voice. Nathan shrugged.

"I hear you've been seeing men in your room at night. Well, you know, the same thing happened to me when I was your age. I saw people all the time in my room at night. I even saw a wolf."

That sparked interest in Nathan. He looked up at Steve. "A wolf?"

Steve nodded. "He turned out to be one of my teachers."

"Really?"

"Really."

Steve lifted his hands and held them palms out towards Nathan. "Rub your hands together, then put your hands out like mine and tell me if you feel this."

Nathan put his hands out, his palms an inch away from Steve's. Steve gently sent his energy out towards Nathan. A look of surprise illuminated the boy's face. "You feel that?"

"Yeah!" Nathan exclaimed.

"I bet you feel a lot of people's energies, don't you? If your friend is sad or your teacher is upset, you know it, don't you?" Nathan nodded solemnly. "Sometimes you feel different because you can feel that stuff." Nathan hesitated, then nodded again. "Well, I'm here to tell you that you're not different. A lot of people feel stuff like that. In fact, my whole group feels people's emotions the same way you do."

Nathan looked at each of us, awestruck by this revelation.

"Would you like me to show you something you can do when all that energy starts making you feel yucky?"

"Sure."

He explained to the little boy how to ground, using the red ball under his feet technique (see Chapter One). He then had Nathan stand up and did a little healing on Nathan's belly, allowing the boy to feel the nervous energy move down his legs and out of the bottom of his feet.

"Can you feel the energy moving into the ground?"

"Yeah! That's cool."

"Excellent! You can do that anytime you want." Now that he had Nathan's confidence, Steve turned to the reason why we were there.

"Your mom tells us you can't sleep because of the men in your room. Do you want to tell us about it?"

"They wake me up at night."

"Do they make a noise?"

He nodded. "Sometimes they do. Sometimes they just walk through without saying anything at all."

"What do they look like?"

"A couple have rags tied around their heads. They look dirty and tired. Some have blood on them. Sometimes they cry."

"Can you see how they're dressed?"

He cocked his head for a moment. "They're dressed kind of funny. It's like they have stockings on. Some of them anyway. Not all of them."

"Can you show us where you see them?"

Nathan climbed off the couch and led us down a long corridor. At the end, we turned to the left and entered his bedroom. It was a typical boy's room, filled with toy cars and trucks and posters of the latest movie action heroes adorning the walls.

We noticed that his room faced the front of the house. He pointed to his closet which lay opposite the windows. "They come out of my closet. Then they walk in front of my bed and go out my window. Only it's like the window isn't there. They just walk through it."

So far we'd felt nothing to indicate the physical presence of a ghost. There was no emotion, no pain, nothing. But Nathan's vivid description certainly showed something was going on.

We closed our eyes to concentrate, trying to tap into what we'd already concluded was a residual haunting. I had a clue as to what was going on, but decided for the moment to remain silent. Becky confirmed my suspicions when she opened her eyes and pointed towards the closet.

"I get a sense of a troop of men. They look like they're from the colonial era. They're exhausted and stumbling after each other. Some look wounded. Others are helping the wounded."

She started taking pictures of the closet area. "The poor men look so done in," she continued.

"So there really are ghosts in my room?" Nathan asked.

"Yes and no," Steve said. He laughed when he saw Nathan's quizzical look. "Have you ever burned yourself with a match or something like that?" The boy thought about it for a moment, then nodded.

"Yeah, once."

"Did it leave a mark?"

"Yeah."

"Okay, that's sort of what's happening here. These men that you're seeing suffered a trauma. Something that so affected them emotionally that it actually left a mark in the air, just like your burn left a mark on your skin. They're not really here, but their memory is here. Does that make sense?"

"Kinda." He tucked his head, but glanced at us shyly through his bangs. "Can you make them go away?"

"We're going to try our best."

We left Nathan and Becky, who was still taking pictures in the bedroom and pulled Abby outside into the corridor to speak with her privately.

"We have two things going on here," Steve explained. "The first is that your son is an empath." His eyes twinkled. "And I'll bet you are too because these things usually run in families."

Abby paused for a moment, then nodded. "That's true. I do feel everything. I try to shut it out as much as I can, but sometimes it's tough."

Steve had her go through the grounding exercise he'd shown Nathan earlier. She was delighted at how quickly and efficiently it worked.

"I don't think we'll have a problem moving the residual energy out," he continued. "However, since Nathan is still too young to understand what being an empath is all about, I'm going to say a prayer that will allow him time to grow up and live a life before he takes on these responsibilities. I'm also going to place warrior angels in the four corners of the house to look after him until such time that he won't need them anymore."

"Warrior angels?" Abby questioned.

"They work for Archangel Michael, who's the angel of protection. They're pretty good at looking after children like Nathan who aren't quite ready to embrace their abilities."

"So who are those men he's seeing?"

I stepped forward. "Do you know about Arlington's role in the beginning of the Revolutionary War?"

Abby shook her head.

The Revolutionary War

In the past, I had served as a tour guide for the National Minuteman Park in Concord, Massachusetts, regaling audiences with the story of what occurred there. I now fell back into my tour guide role to tell Abby what we believed was going on in Nathan's room.

"On April 19, 1775, the British marched out to Concord to retrieve what they believed were munitions being stockpiled by the colonials. Along the way, they encountered troops of minutemen determined to fight them off. Shots were fired, first in Lexington and then in Concord where the battle grew more heated. The British now had

After we set the angels, the sky is filled with multi-colored orbs.

Before we set angels to protect Nathan, the sky is empty.

to make it back to their headquarters in Boston where they'd be safe. They started what we refer to as the 'running battle'; it was basically a mad dash back to Boston through various towns. The colonials followed them every step of the way, picking the British off from behind trees and stone fences. The worst of the fighting took place here in Arlington. At the time, the town was known as Menotomy. Because of the closely packed houses, the fighting grew intense and the worst casualties on both sides took place here. I'll do some more research, but I'm convinced that what your son is seeing is the emotional imprint of the colonials staggering back through Arlington on that day."

Abby nodded as she listened to my story. When I was done, we formed our prayer circle. Steve called upon Guidance to watch over Nathan and allow him a respite in order to grow up and understand the gifts he'd been given. We cleared the residual energy of the soldiers and placed the four angels around the house to keep Nathan and his family free from feeling any more of the trauma that had once bloodied Arlington's streets.

Follow-Up:

Leaving Abby and Nathan, we were drawn to continue deeper into the town of Arlington. There, on a main street, we pulled over and found ourselves in front of a plaque that told the story of Arlington's place in history on April 19, 1776. The area where Abby and Nathan's house is located was the scene of the colonials' retreat after the skirmishes that took place in Arlington. There were reports of many bloodied and battered men marching through there after the British retreated.

The prayers said to give Nathan the time necessary to grow up were successful, as were the angels placed to watch over the family. As of this writing, there have been no more reports of soldiers marching through Nathan's bedroom and he is leading a happy, rambunctious life.

What Does it Mean to be an Empath?

Empath is the name given to an individual who is basically a human sponge, feeling everyone's emotions, whether it is through personal interactions or on a global scale. Many people consider this a curse, but it's a blessing when you consider that the job of an empath is to change the energy that they're feeling. Every thought, every emotion that a human being experiences goes out into the air. If a person had a bad life, what happens? That energy goes out. If they had a good life, that energy goes out as well. An empath who feels all that energy has two choices. They can medicate themselves so they don't feel anything anymore, or they can learn to deal with it through the process of grounding. Because this is something that is not talked about much, people who feel so much tend to "own it." In other words, they don't move the energy and it clings to them, weighing them down, especially if it's a frenetic or depressing energy. (Think about feeling everyone's emotions in a mall during the holiday season.) However, it doesn't matter if the emotions an empath is feeling are their own or someone else's. The idea is to ground out the energy to increase their own personal vibration. The more they increase their vibration, the more they increase their ability to love. And that love reverberates out. It's like a pebble thrown out into the water. It causes a ripple effect. As an empath, a person can change the energy around them by raising its vibration.

When it comes to dealing with spirits, it is important to remember that everything is energy, including our own. Each human being comes to this life to learn certain lessons. It's like climbing a stairway. Each lesson you learn, you go up a step. What happens if a person didn't live the life they were supposed to live? They don't reach that threshold that allows them to see the Door at the time of death. So what does that spirit do? They wander, looking for the energy that they feel most comfortable with. For example, if a person died an alcoholic, they're going to seek out the living who are alcoholics because that's the energy they're comfortable with. As a living person, if you feel a spirit around you, (and you will know if you suddenly find yourself feeling emotions that you weren't feeling a few moments before), you can go through those emotions for them. It needs repeating that ghosts no longer have a body to process those emotions, but we do. We open our hearts, change those old emotions they're still holding onto by moving the energy through us. It brings them up to that threshold and once they reach it, they can go through the Door. You can't destroy energy. You can only raise its vibration.

4

The House That Hated People

O N A BUSY ROAD IN SOUTHERN NEW HAMPSHIRE SITS A HOUSE, its front walk shaded by centuries-old trees. It's easy to miss if you drive by – just another old farmhouse in a neighborhood of old farmhouses. But this house is different. If its history is any indication, this is a house that appears to hate its tenants.

Grace Michaels, an elegant, attractive woman in her early 40s, had acquired the house as an investment. She planned to turn the multi-room, multi-storied house into rental property. Grace, who is a believer in the paranormal, never expected that her 100-year-old farmhouse would turn out to be so deadly.

Through a succession of tenants, it slowly dawned on her that something was wrong with the house. How to explain tenants who, once they moved in, would find their lives turned upside down, bedeviled with illness, loss of job, or strange accidents. Her first set of tenants left when the children became inexplicably ill. The second set, a successful legal firm, found itself facing bankruptcy within six months of moving into the house. The third set saw the break-up of what had been, up until the time of moving in, a happy, successful marriage. Her last tenants, a family of seven, moved out six months after the husband suddenly lost his job, his health, and became convinced there was "something" in the house causing it all. Their convictions were aided by strange sounds at night, lights turning off and on, footsteps stomping downstairs when everyone was in bed. Yet the most terrifying apparition was a shadowy fog that would suddenly appear, then just as quickly disappear. The frightened husband told Grace that whenever the fog appeared, an oppression would settle over him, a darkness that encouraged him to end it all and commit suicide. Or worse. To hurt his wife and children.

They left in the middle of the night, taking nothing but themselves and a few articles of clothing.

Realizing what she had on her hands, Grace refused to rent to anyone else until she could figure out what to do about the deadly goings-on. The house had been empty for several months before she heard about us through a friend. She immediately called Steve and set up an appointment for us to visit the house and get to the bottom of the mystery.

Not Tinkerbell

We arrived on a windy, rainswept night tailor-made for a horror movie. On that evening, the team consisted of Steve, David, Joy and me. We drove by the house twice before we finally found ourselves pulling into a long, weed-choked driveway to an old circa-1800s farmhouse set back from the main road.

With tires rumbling over the muddy driveway, we noticed an air of sadness about the three-story, white clapboard building — as if it had once known good times, but its happiness was now overshadowed by memories too terrible to remember.

The rain was coming down in buckets. We saw Grace's minivan already parked in the driveway and the light was on in the kitchen. Before any of us could move, we felt our chests tightening. This is our indication that we are dealing with a lower vibrational energy. Because of all the personal work we've done as individuals to heal and discard those emotions and traumas that no longer serve us, our vibrations have risen. When we come in contact with a spirit whose energy is lower, it's like oil and vinegar. They just don't mix.

"We haven't even gone inside the farmhouse yet and I already want to throw up," I remarked as I gathered my equipment and made ready to dash through the rain.

"You know any house that's going to chase out four different sets of tenants isn't going to be fun and games," Steve responded.

"Once in a while it wouldn't hurt to investigate a house that's haunted by Tinkerbell. Or Winnie the Pooh."

"Ah, those are boring. Unless of course Winnie the Pooh is actually demonic or Tinkerbell is a succubus."

I laughed. Steve was right. We *did* enjoy the sinister investigations.

Grace had the door open for us. We ran inside and immediately felt the off-kilter energy.

"I'm so glad you could make it out on such a miserable night," Grace replied as she started walking us through the house. "Please be careful as you walk along. I've been trying to clean up but there's still so much to do."

The rooms were lit with single light bulbs suspended from the ceiling, sending out feeble shadows as we slowly walked through the downstairs, cameras and recorders in hand. We were instantly astonished to see just how quickly the last tenants had departed. Everywhere we looked, we saw piles of discarded clothing, children's toys, furniture and half empty suitcases. It looked as though they'd been chased out, taking nothing but the clothes on their backs.

"I wasn't quite sure what to believe," Grace explained as she led us from room to room. "I'd never heard about this fog that appears on the stairway. At first I thought it was their imaginations. Then, last week I was here by myself. It was after dark and I was upstairs on the third floor. At one time they were bedrooms, then used as storage space. I decided to convert them back to bedrooms. I was mopping down the floor when I started getting a strong sensation of being watched. I couldn't shake it no matter what I did. I tried my best to ignore it. The fact that the house is old and creaky and I was here by myself made me think I was just imagining things. But the feeling just got stronger and stronger. Finally, I couldn't stand it anymore. I decided to call it a night and turned to go downstairs." She hesitated.

"What happened?" Steve prompted.

"I saw the fog. It stood right at the top of the stairs. If I'd wanted to leave, I would have had to go right through it. I was trapped and absolutely terrified. I can't remember how long I stood staring at it. It hovered above the floor before finally disappearing. One minute it was there, and the next minute it was gone. But before it disappeared, I felt such a deep sense of despair and hopelessness." She shuddered. "I never want to feel those emotions again."

Joy and I exchanged glances. This was the kind of investigation we loved.

We finished covering the first and second floors, finding more signs of a hasty retreat by the previous tenants. There were also signs of Grace's clean-up efforts. Clothes were neatly piled up in corners and toys were stacked, ready to be taken away.

We climbed the stairs to the third floor. A lone light bulb hung from a string in the middle of the long hallway. It sent out eerie shadows against the walls and corners, making it easy to see how anyone could be spooked being up there alone.

With the rain beating against the windows, we poked our heads into three bedrooms that branched off the corridor. They were empty of furnishings and clothing and the air smelled of disinfectant and wood polish.

Entering the last bedroom at the end of the corridor, we saw a perfectly square room with peeling wallpaper and a rich walnut floor. Joy and David walked over to the windows and peered through the raindrops weaving paths down the outside glass. I watched them cock their heads for a moment.

"I'm hearing children playing," David said.

"Me too," Joy concurred. She pointed towards the left of the window. "It sounds like a crowd of children and it feels like it's coming from over there."

Grace nodded. "You can't see it right now because of the rain, but there's a school next door. The playground abuts my property."

We had no prior knowledge of the house or the surrounding area, so we were happy with the confirmation.

"As you can see, these rooms need a lot of TLC. I was planning on hiring contractors to come in and tear down the wallpaper and redo the walls. But I don't want to invest any more money until we get whatever is going on here resolved."

"That makes sense," Steve agreed.

We retraced our steps back down the corridor and entered the next bedroom. This one was on the opposite side of the house, looking away from the school. Grace hesitated on the threshold. "I don't know why, but this room in particular disturbs me. I never feel comfortable in it."

David and Joy walked to the center of the room and stood quietly, eyes closed, concentrating. Steve, Grace, and I stood to the side and watched.

"Somebody died in this room," Joy announced.

"Well, the place is over 100 years old. I wouldn't be surprised if people did die in here," Grace replied.

"No, it's more than someone dying. I'm feeling hands around my throat."

Grace gave a start.

"Let's keep looking," Steve spoke up, seeing Grace's reaction. "There's more going on here."

We entered the third and last bedroom located directly opposite the staircase. Once again the wallpaper was peeling, and on the far wall, water damage had torn away the wallpaper and stained the wall underneath. Joy was in front of me and I almost crashed into her when she suddenly came to a complete stop.

"I just walked into something!" she exclaimed. The room was empty, so we couldn't figure out what she was talking about. That is, until she put her hand out and let out another gasp. "Oh my God! Feel this!"

Each of us put our hands out and were amazed to find our fingers touching a mass of energy hovering above the floor about eye-level.

The energy ball could not be seen by the naked eye, but we could feel energy swirling in and around it. Our best guess was that it was about the size of a basketball.

"What is that?" I asked Steve.

"I'm not sure yet."

At that moment, those of us who were facing the door caught a dark blur move past the doorway and down the corridor. We ran outside, but whatever it was had disappeared. We returned to the energy ball and found that it was still there. We debated what it could be, but as the hour grew late, we decided to finish up taking pictures and EVPs. We promised Grace we would return the next week to continue the investigation.

A Choking Experience

A week later, the energy ball was still there. While taking pictures outside, I suddenly felt something or someone walk up behind me. I quickly turned around and captured a dark shadow standing at my left shoulder.

Despite this shadow, we felt the key to the haunting lay in the room where Joy had felt the hands around her throat. We gathered in that bedroom and began to "tune in." It wasn't long before we were all feeling the sensation of hands around our throats.

Joy shuddered and grabbed my hand. "There's been abuse here," she said. "With children."

The temperature gauge in Joy's hand suddenly dropped ten degrees and we found ourselves enveloped in an icy blanket of air.

"Somebody just walked in, didn't they?" Grace asked, her eyes wide with fear as she glanced around the empty room.

What was this dark shadow and orb hovering around Grace's house?

Steve nodded. "What happened here?" he asked aloud.

"I'm seeing an old woman in a bed against this wall," Joy replied, her eyes tightly shut as she tried to decipher what she was seeing.

The energy spiked. "What is it about this woman that's angering this spirit?" Steve asked.

"I'm getting that it's her son," Joy continued.

David slowly let out his breath. "My God, he really hates her."

The sensation of choking once more made itself known. "I think he choked his mother," I replied.

"But why?"

Joy began to gently rock back and forth. "She abused him."

At that moment, the room grew colder. Grace's eyes grew even wider with anxiety and trepidation.

"And he in turn abused others in this house," Steve finished.

The room seemed to shudder as the secrets of the farmhouse were revealed.

"Dear God," Grace whispered under her breath.

"The energy ball is a collection of all the dysfunction and misery that's taken place since the abuse happened," Steve explained.

"So the old woman and her son are still here and they're responsible for what's been happening?" Grace asked.

This photo, snapped seconds after the photo above shows the dark shadow and orb gone.

"Yes. They're anchoring that heavy energy here and are keeping people from discovering their secrets by terrorizing them. Let's do a prayer circle. Bety, you want to lead the prayer on this one?"

I nodded and closed my eyes to center myself. I felt the words in my heart and began to gently repeat them.

> Creator, we stand before you, hands to hands and hearts to hearts in a place that has seen much pain, much misunderstanding, much misery. The mother dealt with the son in the only way she knew how, remembering how her mother had dealt with her. The son, in agony and loathing, took out that agony and loathing on others who were as innocent as he once had been. We ask that this space be cleared of all those energies that did not serve then and which do not serve now. We ask that you allow this woman who now owns this property to rent a home that now knows peace. We ask that the mother and son enter our circle and understand that we do not hold you in judgment, nor in contempt. You did the best you could with what you knew. Know that you can leave this place, no longer bound by guilt and loathing and hatred. Know that a better place awaits you where you can find the peace you could not find in life or death. Go to Creator and continue your journey.

Our bodies filled with loathing, anger, shame and guilt, the emotions the mother and son had been holding on to for so many years. Trapped in their neverending drama, these sentiments, so dense and heavy, prevented them from moving on towards the Light. We took on their emotions, grounding them through our feet. It wasn't long before we felt their spirits lighten, no longer burdened with the weight of their feelings. By the time I was done, the pall that had hung over the house was gone. We inspected each room in the house. They were clean, no longer filled with the oppression that had once inhabited its walls. To our amazement, when we went in search of the energy ball, we found that it too was gone.

Follow-up

After our visit, Grace reported that she was now able to stay in the house alone without fear and without the feeling that she was being watched. She brought in contractors and completely redid both the inside and outside of the building. Soon after its completion, she found new tenants who instantly fell in love with the house. As of this writing, several years later, there have been no more runs of "bad luck" in the old farmhouse.

Centering Yourself

If you feel yourself losing control of your emotions and grounding isn't enough, try centering yourself by doing the following: Close your eyes and imagine the top of your head as the top of a triangle. Your left and right hands are the left and right sides of the triangle. The bottom of the triangle runs along your belly. Now focus on the top of the triangle. It may actually feel that it's not centered over the top of your head. If it isn't, gently push the top of the triangle until it's resting right above the crown of your head. Once you've gotten the top of the triangle centered over your head, imagine white light pouring into the top of the triangle, down into your body. What you are doing is establishing a connection back to Source. Now take all this white light and ground it out the bottom of your feet. You should start to feel yourself centered and balanced. Reconnect to Source during the day so you stay in the flow of energy.

5

This Is My House

I WAS AT WORK ONE MORNING, trying to concentrate on the financial spreadsheet staring out at me from my work computer. My eyes were swimming; I'd been trying to find an error in a calculation and I'd been at it for almost two hours. When my cell phone rang, I was more than grateful for the interruption. "Don't Fear the Reaper" by Blue Oyster Cult filled my office space as I grabbed my cell. The tune was my attempt at paranormal investigation humor. Why fear the reaper when we know life after death exists? I looked at the caller I.D. and saw it was Steve.

"What's up?" I asked.

"I just got a call from Ron. He's referring a case to us."

Ron was Ron Kolek from the New England Ghost Project, a paranormal investigative team that operates out of Dracut, Massachusetts. We'd been friendly for years, especially since my close friend, Maureen Wood, was the team's psychic medium. Because of our reputation for taking on the darker cases, we were occasionally asked by other paranormal teams to help them out on some of their hairier investigations.

"His group was investigating a house in Hartford, Connecticut, when he was physically knocked to the floor by an unseen presence. He thought the energy there was demonic and has asked us to see what we can do to help the family. Apparently, they've also been suffering from physical attacks and need help ASAP."

I smiled. "I'll gather the troops and tell them to bring the extra heavy armor."

Get Out!

It was a warm summer day as Steve, Amy, Becky, Lisa, and I drove the two hours to the outskirts of Hartford. On the way, as happens many times when we're en route to an investigation, we began to perceive bits and pieces of information that, at the moment, made no sense, but would become clearer as the day wore on.

"This is going to sound a little crazy," Amy remarked as she shook her head from side to side.

"You honestly think we'd find anything crazy?" Steve joked as he stretched his long legs out in front of him, not an easy thing to do in a Prius.

Amy laughed. "True. I keep seeing a lion. It reminds me of Aslan, the lion from the *Chronicles of Narnia.* Only angrier. He's so vivid. He's just standing there, looking at me and showing his teeth."

"Well, tell him to move. You're driving and I'm not quite ready to find myself on the Other Side just yet," I piped up from the backseat.

"Is the lion saying anything to you?" Becky asked. "Any messages or warnings?"

Amy's eyes looked inward and I prayed she could communicate with her spirit guides and drive at the same time. I know we're very well protected, but I didn't see any sense in pushing it. I sighed with relief when she seemingly came out of it and shook her head. "Nope. Just an angry lion staring me down."

"I'd rather have your vision," Steve quipped. "Right now, I'm feeling myself surrounded by tentacles."

"Like an octopus's tentacles?" Lisa asked.

"Exactly. The energy of whatever this thing is feels awful. Don't know who or what it means yet."

As Steve spoke, the car grew colder. Whatever was at this house knew we were on our way. Were these visions warnings to us to stay away?

We had no problem finding the small white clapboard house. It lay off the main thoroughfare in the middle of industrial warehouses. Surrounded by a chain link fence, it sat in a neighborhood of identical houses – testimony to the frenzy of small suburban house building that took place shortly after the end of World War II to accommodate the returning GIs.

We parked across the street in an empty lot and found Joy and David, who had recently started the Connecticut chapter of the Spirit Light Network, waiting for us. Piling out of the Prius, we all stood together and looked around, trying to get a feel for the place. The surrounding homes were neat and clean, but it was obvious that the neighborhood itself had seen better days. Everything looked rundown, as if the inhabitants were only able to keep up with the most basic of repairs and maintenance.

We crossed the street towards the house. Immediately, several members of the team were struck by the ghostly presence of an elderly man in his 60s. Short, and squat with tattoos on his arms and a snarly look on his grizzled face, he sat on the front concrete steps and silently watched us approach. Drawing closer, we were assailed by the strong scent of tobacco and beer.

"GET OUT!" the spirit growled menacingly.

I turned to the others. "Tell me I'm not the only one who heard that."

The others nodded. "Nope," Steve replied. "We heard it, too."

"Sounds like this is going to be a fun one," Becky murmured as Steve rang the doorbell. We heard the yapping of several small dogs, then the door was opened by a heavy, middle-aged woman with long, curly blond hair that came down to her shoulders. She was dressed in a navy blue top and jeans and seemed genuinely glad to see us. She introduced herself as Cindy as she ushered us into a small living room that lay to the left of a staircase that led up the second floor.

The living room itself was dark and gloomy. Despite the beautiful summer day outside, the shades were tightly drawn. The dark paneling on the wall made the room appear even darker. It gave the impression of a family keeping something out.

Or was something being kept in?

The room itself was small, made smaller by all the furniture crammed into its tiny space. It was difficult for us to stand together and we tried to spread out so we wouldn't trip over each other, or step on the three fluffy Shih-tzus that were bouncing and barking around our ankles.

We were introduced to Cindy's daughter, Karen, who also seemed very happy to see us. The spitting image of her mother, Karen looked to be about eighteen.

Thankfully, the living room opened out into a spacious kitchen. We instantly made our way towards it. Just as we were about to enter, a young man appeared in the doorway. He was dressed in black and kept his face averted from us, his long dark brown bangs helping to keep his features hidden. Cindy introduced him as her son, Randy. He appeared to be in his early twenties. Without looking up, he grunted a greeting.

We looked at Randy, then at each other. In our mind's eye, we saw him surrounded by a suffocating dark cloud of energy. Drawing nearer to him, the darkness became more impenetrable, more foreboding. Our hearts clenched and our stomachs tightened, a telltale sign that what was surrounding Randy was not good. His energy felt as though it were mired in sludge. When he finally peeked at us through his bangs, we could see that he was either hung over or still under the effects of drugs or heavy medication.

Arranging ourselves in the kitchen, I noticed that Randy deliberately sat as far away from us as possible. His arms were tightly crossed against his chest and his feet were in constant motion, tap, tap, tapping against the floor. His eyes roamed everywhere.

Except at us.

Cindy started to share her story. However, I was forced to excuse myself to use the bathroom. A two-hour trip from Massachusetts, with a side visit to grab a cup of coffee will do that.

Karen took me back to the living room and pointed out a door under the stairs. I ducked inside. All the while I was in there, I wondered how we were going to help Randy. What was attached to him had nothing to do with the spirit of the man we'd encountered when we arrived. Randy's problem was much more immediate. And serious.

Preoccupied as I was, I gave a startled jump when I glanced in the mirror and caught the unexpected image of a young girl standing behind me. I whirled around. She was gone, but I could feel her energy in the room with me.

Although the sighting had been brief, I was able to recall in vivid detail what she looked like. She was young, about the same age as Karen. She had long straight raven black hair, heavy dark eye make-up, and was dressed in 1980s punk-era clothes – ripped jeans and t-shirt held together by safety pins. Although her clothes gave the impression of a tough demeanor, her energy spoke of a person who had been sweet and poignantly innocent.

"Who are you?" I asked her under my breath.

"I'm still waiting for him," I heard the silvery whisper in my head. "Why won't he come? He told me he loved me." Her words were couched in such longing and desperation that it broke my heart.

"Who are you waiting for?"

"My boyfriend. He told me he's coming. Where is he?"

I didn't respond. What could I say? I left the bathroom and found Amy waiting to use it. When she was done, she came up to me and pulled me aside. "Did you see the girl in the bathroom mirror?"

I nodded. "Did she say anything to you?" I asked.

"She's desperate to be with her boyfriend. She's waiting for him to come back."

We hoped we'd find out more as the visit progressed.

While Lisa and Steve spoke with the family, the rest of us fanned out. Becky, Joy, and David went upstairs while Amy and I stepped back into the living room. The spirit of the angry man who had met us outside now reappeared. His turbulent, proprietary energy swirled around us, making it clear this was his house and he didn't enjoy us being there. Amy and I ignored him as we made our way back towards the bathroom. I'd noticed a small bedroom tucked back there and was curious to check it out. We stepped into the bedroom and noticed right away that the angry man had not entered with us.

The bedroom, painted in a soft blue, held a full-size bed and a bureau with a mirror. On the bureau, in a silver frame, was the photograph of a man in his late forties. Judging by his clothing, the picture appeared to have been taken recently. Amy looked at the picture and shivered a little. "I can feel him in this room," she said, pointing at the photo. "Funny how the man in the living room is nasty, but this man is all about love and protection."

"Maybe that's why he hangs around in this room. If I had to deal with Mr. Personality out there, I'd stay in here, too."

An Unhealthy Discovery

The next stop was the basement. This was where Ron had been knocked down and we were anxious to see what we could find.

Steve opted to follow us down a rickety set of stairs while Lisa stayed in the kitchen to continue counseling the family.

Reaching the bottom of the steps, we were overcome with the sharp scent of cat urine. It permeated the entire area. What was strange was that at no time during our walkthrough had we encountered any cats, litter boxes, feed or water bowls. We involuntarily gagged and covered our noses with our hands.

The basement was divided into two parts. The first part at the bottom of the stairs held the washer/dryer and various storage boxes piled and stacked all over each other. At the far end of the room was a set of beaded curtains. Beyond that was a closed door. We snapped off pictures as best we could; then, with Amy leading the way, we went through the beaded curtains and opened the door.

We unexpectedly found ourselves in a bedroom that we quickly surmised belonged to Randy. A twin-size bed was up against the wall. Next to it was a stack of CDs on a bureau and a guitar resting against the bed. With a television and a couch, he'd essentially created a mini-apartment for himself. However, the dead giveaway that it was Randy's room was the array of pictures of nude women tacked up on the entire wall next to the bed. I turned away, a little embarrassed by the graphic nature of many of the photos. The odor of cat urine wasn't as strong, but it was still in the air.

"Will you look at this," Amy smiled as she walked up to the opposite wall. I looked up and caught my breath.

Set between a poster of a Bengal tiger and one of Marilyn Monroe, there was a drawing on the pressboard wall of a huge male lion, its paws outstretched as if it was ready to attack.

"I think we found Aslan," she said. "The drawing looks exactly like the vision I had in the car."

Steve drew closer to study it. "Randy's mother said he barely leaves this room," he said as he stretched his hand out to touch the drawing.

There was a palpable darkness shrouding the room. It matched the darkness we'd felt surrounding Randy. It had nothing to do with the pornography on the walls, nor with the magnificent drawing of the lion. The very air we stood in was crushing, as if it could squeeze the breath from our lungs. There was also a sense of warning. Whatever was in this room didn't want us in there. The sense of someone or something staring at us was unshakeable. I couldn't imagine spending any time in this room, much less the night. The oppressiveness was suffocating. I took a step back and started to snap pictures.

"How could anyone live down here?" Joy wondered aloud, echoing our thoughts. "There's something so *dark* in this room." She shuddered.

"Damn. I can feel those tentacles again," Steve announced.

As Steve said a prayer, these tentacles were captured on film trying to stop him.

At that moment I snapped a picture, When I looked at it, I was stunned. "Hey guys, look at this."

I turned the digital display on my camera so everyone could see the image I'd captured. "My hair's too short to have swung into the lens. And none of you were around me when I took it." I looked up at Steve. "Looks like we captured those tentacles right at the moment you were feeling them."

"What do you think it is?" Becky asked.

Steve stared down at the photo. "I'd say it's the demon Randy has attached to him."

We looked at Steve. Despite the tendency of many ghost investigators, especially those on television, to claim everything is a demon, the truth is demons are not that prevalent. Many times the darkness surrounding a place or a person is simply an angry ghost. We'd investigated countless places where other investigators swore a demon was running amok, only to discover it was just an angry or malevolent dead guy. This, however, was different. The energy haunting Randy truly was demonic.

"A demon with tentacles?" Becky questioned.

"A demon will use whatever it can to hold on."

"You know," Joy said, "I thought I read somewhere that the sharp odor of cat urine where there are no signs of cats, can indicate the presence of a demon."

With all fingers pointing to the probability of a demon overshadowing Randy, Steve closed his eyes and began to intone a prayer. We felt the darkness in the room back away from us, but it refused to leave.

"It's not going anywhere as long as Randy remains in the state he's in," Steve said when he saw our disappointed faces. "Even if we got it to go, it would only come back. And if not this particular demon, then another."

"But there has to be *something* we can do. I hate leaving it here," Becky replied.

"This is a situation where the living is contributing to this thing being here. Randy is too good a meal for the demon to be pushed away from. Cindy says he enjoys the dark side of things. He doesn't want help. I could tell by his attitude upstairs he hates us being here."

We reluctantly left Randy's room and quickly made our way upstairs, grateful to be away from the sickening odors and the blackness in his room.

More Ghosts

"Have you finished checking out the house?" Steve asked.

"No," Amy responded. "Bety and I haven't gone upstairs yet."

"Why don't you do that? I'll check in and see how Lisa's doing."

While he remained in the kitchen with Lisa and the family, the rest of us climbed the stairs to what was essentially an empty room under the eaves. There were two storage bins and an old dresser, but nothing else to indicate that anyone used this room for anything other than storage.

We took advantage of the quiet space and sat down in a circle. If we were going to communicate with the spirits, this was the best place to do it in.

The darkness in Randy's room had remained downstairs, but we were soon joined by Mr. Personality. He swooped in and we were once again enveloped in his frigidly cold, quarrelsome energy.

"I'll bet you this is the guy responsible for knocking Ron down and physically assaulting the family," David said as the spirit circled us.

"It makes sense that he would attack the family. He still considers this his house and he doesn't want them in here," I mused. "As for

The group prepares to make contact with angry spirit nicknamed Mr. Personality.

Amy working with her mesa to try and calm Mr. Personality down.

Ron, he does have a tendency to antagonize a spirit to get a reaction. Mr. Personality feels like the type who would knock somebody down if he didn't like what was said."

We took turns reaching out to the angry male spirit, reassuring him we meant him no harm. We encouraged him to tell us his story, but he was extremely distrustful. Just as we were at our wits end, Amy came up with a plan that we hoped would work.

Amy has been privileged to travel to Peru and study with several indigenous shamans. She has undergone several Peruvian shaman rites and carries with her at all times a mesa. This is a cloth in which her healing stones and other articles she uses in her ceremonies are kept. They retain the power and high intentions of her rites and healing sessions. She took a moment to unwrap her mesa and spread the stones out in a grid. The purpose was to create a space where the owner of the home would feel safe and calm enough to enter our circle and make contact with us.

We waited while she spread the stones and said a prayer. When she was done, we held hands.

"Here's your chance to tell us why you're here and why you don't want anyone in your house," I announced. "We mean you no harm, nor does anyone who lives here. You're frightening them."

There was silence. Just as we thought Amy's technique had failed, I felt my left arm freeze.

"The woman is a slut!" he shouted in my left ear. *"She's fat! She's a slob! She's a bitch!"*

I repeated to the others what I was hearing. Before he could escalate further, I interrupted. "Why are you holding on? What is it that you want us to know? What can we do to help you?"

He came up next to me and it took me a moment to realize he was trying to meld his energy with mine. I knew he wanted to get inside and use my body and voice to communicate. I was leery about allowing him to speak through me. He was obviously an angry, manipulative being and I wasn't sure I wanted that energy inside me.

At the same time, I wanted to help this spirit move on and leave this family in peace. We weren't sure if we could do anything about the demon attached to Randy, but we could try our best to move the other spirits out of the house.

Whenever I channel, I remain conscious throughout the process. It's like sitting in the back of the room. I hear what is being said, even though it's rare I remember much of it.

If channeling this man would give the family a chance at tranquility, it was worth a shot. Having made my decision, I carefully opened myself up. I felt his energy come in sideways, as if he'd taken a step to the left and stepped into me. I felt my body morph into that of a heavyset man with whiskers on my chin and brawny muscles on my arms. I could smell the odor of tobacco and stale beer ooze from my pores. A flash of images shot through my brain.

"I'm seeing fire. Explosions. I'm hearing men screaming," I said as I tried to interpret the pictures I was seeing. "It feels like war."

I shook my head as I felt a strong emotion settle in my heart. It was so deep, so profound that I found myself blinking back tears. I allowed my conscious mind to take a step back and my mouth moved as he began to speak.

Why did I come back when they didn't? Why did I survive? I lost friends dammit. Fine men who should have had a life. It should have been me.

I was overcome with a guilt so heartfelt, it almost crushed me. The images in my mind shifted and I saw him sitting with a group of men in the middle of a forest. They were dressed in the uniforms of World War II soldiers. I watched as he cradled the bodies of dying men, then fast forwarding to his life after the service when he began to drink. His verbal abuse of his wife and son. His deliberate shutting away in this house, bitter and angry and guilt-stricken that he'd been spared. And the worse emotion of all – rage at himself for squandering the life that he'd been given while his friends' lives were taken away.

The part of me that was still conscious was overcome with compassion. I heard Joy speaking gently to him, trying to persuade him to forgive himself. Becky and David joined in. Slowly his anger became to dissipate.

We held hands. Our energies joined, our vibrations rose. A white light appeared in the far corner of the room and started to build. It soon reached our circle, immersing us in its twinkling, shimmering light. We gave a collective gasp as we realized it was his friends, still dressed in their uniforms, gathering around to take him home. I heard the sounds of sniffling around me and I realized we were all crying as we watched these soldiers take him by the hand and draw him away to a place where he could be with his buddies again. I could hear them encouraging him, joking with him. I saw him hesitate. Then he took their hands. His energy lifted up and away from me and in the blink of an eye, he was gone.

However, we weren't done yet. The spirit of the girl lingered. Amy connected to her and related her sad story of loving a man who physically abused her until one day the abuse went too far and he killed her. Yet, in her innocence and love, she continued to pine for him, refusing to leave until he came for her. It took us almost twenty minutes to convince her that he wasn't coming back for her. He'd gone on with his own life and it was time for her to move on. Joy said a prayer and with our vibrations humming, she finally stepped over to the Other Side.

It had all been extremely emotional. We remained seated on the floor, wiping our eyes and discussing what we'd just felt. Amy carefully and lovingly put her stones back in her mesa and tied up the cloth. When we were ready, we made our way downstairs to Steve and Lisa, still gathered with the family in the kitchen. We related what we'd found and what we did.

Under Lisa's gentle encouragement, Cindy told us a little about her life. "I know what that young girl went through. I was married to a man who constantly beat me up. I knew he was going to kill me if I didn't get out. So one day I packed my bags, took my kids, and got the hell out of there. It's taken me a while to stop getting involved with abusive men."

"That's why the young girl was here," Steve explained. "This is an example of like energy attracting like energy. Because of your history of getting involved in abusive relationships, the girl was drawn to you because she too was stuck in that abusive energy."

"Do you know anything about the man who owned this place?" Becky asked.

"He died a number of years ago, but my neighbors did tell me a little about him. You're right about the way he treated his wife. He was always yelling at her and tearing her down. He'd sit on the front steps, usually with a beer and a cigarette in his hand, and curse at anyone who walked by. The wife finally got fed up and took off."

"Isn't it interesting that the house you chose to live in also carried the energy of abuse – in this case emotional abuse," Steve pointed out.

Cindy's mouth fell open. "I never thought of that."

"Do you have any idea who the man in the bedroom is?" Amy asked. "His picture is on the dresser."

Cindy nodded as if the news about this third spirit didn't surprise her. "You know, we've always felt Paul is here. You see, that's my sister's room and the picture is of her husband. He suddenly died two months ago of a heart attack."

"He's still looking after her," Amy said.

"I'm sure he is. It's actually been helping Linda, knowing that he's around."

We all felt he knew he could go on, but hadn't chosen to leave yet in order to look after his widow.

However, it was time for us to go. We thanked the family and left. When we were in the car, Lisa provided the rest of the story.

"Randy's been having drug and alcohol problems for a long time now. He's on medication for depression. I spent a lot of time talking to him. I think he listened to me. He seemed to hear and accept what I had to say. Still, he's in such a dark place, I worry about him."

Steve shook his head sadly. "The demon attached to him is feeding off those problems. I wouldn't be surprised if it's keeping him in the emotional mess he's in to continue to feed off him."

"So this isn't a ghost who died an alcoholic or drug addict and is looking for that energy to attach to?" Joy asked.

"It's much darker. The tentacles I felt tell me this is a much more malevolent energy. I get the sense Randy did something to invite this thing in. Ouija board maybe, or simply opening a door that should have stayed closed. That's why his room feels so hopeless."

"Hopefully, he'll get the help he needs," Lisa replied. "I think he wants to. His family certainly wants him to." She shook her head to herself. "He just needs to find the courage to take that first step." She looked at each of us and smiled. "And I'm going to do my part and pray as hard as I can that he finds that strength."

Follow-Up

The house did settle down after our visit. There were no more physical attacks and the atmosphere felt lighter. At least in all the rooms outside of the basement. Unfortunately, we don't know if Randy was able to deal with his personal problems. As of this writing, we continue to send him love and light and wish the best for his recovery.

Attachment and a Primer on Demons

We have found many instances where a living human has actually attracted a wandering soul to themselves because the two share a common denominator. This is known as a spirit attachment. It doesn't matter if the spirit is someone you've never heard of. What's attracting them to you may be something as simple as a shared experience. For example, a person who was an alcoholic in life will be attracted to that energy in death, because that is the energy they are most familiar with. In the above story, the spirit of the young girl was attracted to Cindy because she'd been in abusive relationships and that was the energy the girl knew.

As for demons, they are not as prevalent as is depicted on television. However, they do exist. The following is what we've discovered during investigations regarding these darker entities.

Task-Maskers

This is a name that we gave to entities who appear to us as black-hooded figures. They will attach themselves to people who are going through a fearful, traumatic period in their lives. These are entities that are actually created by *our own fears.* We create them. They feed off our fears, amplify our fears, and try their best to keep us mired in dysfunctionality in order to continue to feed off that energy.

Lower-Energy Demons

The method we use to distinguish between whether a haunting is being caused by an angry spirit or a demon is that a lower-energy demon is one-dimensional. A spirit that was once human will retain human emotions. We will feel their anger, guilt, rage, etc. However, a demon doesn't have those emotions. They will attach themselves to a specific vulnerability of the living. Unlike Task-Maskers, these entities have been in existence since the beginning of time. In Randy's case, his vulnerability was the darker side of his personality that shunned human contact. He created barriers through drugs and alcohol to isolate himself from everyone. This made him a prime target for this particular demon who kept him in that state of apathy and used him to its own end. We have found it's extremely difficult to rid a person of this type of entity unless they make an effort to change. The problem is that the demon will stay away for only so long. Then, if the living person refuses to make the necessary changes to their lives, it will come right back. Unfortunately, until Randy seizes the reins and takes control, this demon will continue to exist around him.

Next Level of Demons

These are stronger demons who have their own agenda and use that agenda to interfere with a person's life path for their own ends. We all come to this Earth with our own life plan – those lessons we need to learn to continue our journey. These demons don't feed off a person's dysfunction so much as actually interfere with their lives. Turn on the television and look at the fear that is sold every day. That collective fear is generating a lot of energy. These demons are feeding the flames of that fear to keep people in a perpetual state of unease. We leak a lot of energy when we react to that fear and take it on ourselves. We also become afraid of taking steps that may actually improve our lives. Who does all this fear benefit? Yet, these demons and task-maskers serve an important purpose. They are there to teach us. We have choices. We can heal. We can turn away from fear and drama. There is a balance to everything. Darkness is simply an absence of light.

Of course not all hauntings have this dynamic taking place. Sometimes a haunting is just a haunting – like Cindy being haunted by the previous owner who didn't like her. Still, it's always beneficial to try and heal those areas of your life that hold you back from achieving true peace and fulfillment. Fear, and the creatures that feed on that fear, are your biggest enemies.

6

At the Cocoanut Grove

M ANY OF OUR INVESTIGATIONS COME FROM WORD OF MOUTH. We investigate one location, clear it of spirits, then find ourselves recommended to friends or family of the original homeowner. Such was the case a few years ago. Steve and I had done an investigation of an old historical mansion, uncovering secrets from the original colonial family that were later confirmed when the caretakers found family diaries detailing the same facts Steve and I had uncovered psychically. Impressed by our abilities, they recommended us to a friend of theirs who had also found a set of diaries dating back to the 1800s. Their friend, Maggie Crosby, convinced that her house was still inhabited by members of the original owners, wanted to make sure they approved of her plan to edit and publish their diaries. She felt the writings would provide valuable insight into daily life at the beginning of the nineteenth century.

It was a nice change of pace not dealing with the spirits of child molesters, murderers, or suicides. Although that is what we're known for, we welcomed a chance to investigate a location where the only thing we were being called upon to do was to psychically connect with a group of spirits to ask if their diaries could be published.

A Shoe-In

It was the height of summer as Steve, Amy, Lisa and I made our way up the New Hampshire shoreline. The sea breezes felt wonderful and when we pulled up to Maggie's house in the small ocean community, we were delighted to find the quintessential New England Victorian mansion. It had a wraparound porch, and its front yard boasted heavily laden flowering hedges. In the back, which stretched out over a hill, Maggie had resurrected the original garden and it was now filled with roses, herbs, sunflowers, and a variety of other brightly colored flora.

A short, middle-aged woman, stylishly dressed and with an open, friendly face greeted us and ushered us through the side of the house and into the kitchen.

"Welcome!" she replied heartily in a patrician accent. "I'm so glad you all could come. I'm looking forward to our time together today."

The kitchen was large, with a counter in the center and beautiful brown and tan tiles on the wall. Off the kitchen, and down a few steps, was a glass-enclosed room where a round table was set for lunch. "I hope you don't mind, but I thought it would be lovely to share a meal."

This was a treat. We usually come in, do our investigation, counsel the family, help release the spirits if they're willing to go, then leave. We're always ravenous after an investigation and it's not unusual for us to be grabbing a slice of pizza at eleven in the evening, since pizzerias seem to be the only places open at such a late hour.

Maggie was a gracious tour guide as she led us through the house, showing off the original architecture with its wainscoting and silk wallpaper. "The house was built in 1802 and I'm the first person outside of the original family to own it. I've been here thirty-five years now."

As in many old houses, the downstairs had large rooms that led into other large rooms. Walking through, we found ourselves in the entrance foyer. Before us lay a wide winding staircase with heavy, highly polished oak banisters. It was pleasant not to feel the constriction in our chests that told us we were dealing with lower energies. On the contrary. The downstairs felt light. The house itself was obviously well cared for and the energy reflected that. We gathered at the foot of the staircase and impressions started to immediately come in.

"I keep seeing shoes," Steve remarked. "The old type with a large buckle on it. And several other styles of shoes."

Maggie smiled, but said nothing.

"There's also a man of authority here. Feels like a judge of some sort. Very stern. Very uncompromising." Steve looked at Maggie. "He's angry about some sort of dispute with the property. Yet his anger isn't overwhelming. He's just not pleased that something didn't go his way. And," Steve added, his blue eyes twinkling, "he was very used to getting his own way."

"Interesting," she said, careful to remain non-committal.

"I'm getting pulled to go into this small room."

"That's my office. Here, I'll take you."

As Steve and Lisa followed Maggie down the corridor towards her office, Amy and I remained standing at the foot of the staircase. Next to me was a round table holding various photographs, some recent, some from the forties and fifties.

"Imagine living in a place like this," I remarked to Amy as I looked at the beautiful wallpaper and rich wood that adorned the walls and staircase.

"This is a beautiful place. And the best part is there are no toys to trip over," she laughed, jokingly referring to her two high-spirited children. Sitting down on the stairway opposite me, she took out her camera and started taking pictures.

Deciding to get out of her way, I moved closer to the table with the photographs. Suddenly, a piercing pain ran through my side and I felt as though my flesh was burning. I yelped and jumped away, accidentally knocking myself against the opposite wall.

"Ow!" I shrieked, as I unconsciously slapped my left side as if to put out a fire that wasn't there.

"Are you alright?" Amy asked, half rising from the stair.

"I feel as though I've just been burned!"

I lifted up the side of my t-shirt, but there were no marks, nothing to indicate what I'd just felt. All I had was the memory of the sharp, searing pain.

"That was weird," I said as I returned to the spot I'd first felt the pain. But nothing happened this time. We searched the foyer, trying to find a possible cause for the burning sensation, but we could find nothing. As I stood there pondering the mystery, Lisa came up and announced that it was time for lunch.

We gathered in the glass-enclosed room off the kitchen and shared a delicious meal of salad, cold pasta, chicken in a cream sauce, and strawberry tarts. Our iced tea was garnished with mint from the garden. Once again, Steve brought up the subject of shoes, telling us that he was still seeing them in his mind's eye even as we ate.

"It's interesting you mention shoes," Maggie replied. "This house was built by two brothers, Isaiah and Joshua Horton, who made their fortune in the shoe business. As you may or may not know, Haverhill, Massachusetts was the site of the shoe industry in New England for many years. Unfortunately, by the third generation, the family had lost most of their money. That's when the dispute with the property occurred. Some of the children wanted to sell, others didn't."

"Where does this judge come in?" Steve asked.

"He was a distant cousin and felt very strongly that the house should not be sold outside the family. Is he one of the spirits who still haunts this place?"

"He feels very protective of this place," Steve responded. "He's happy you're looking after it."

"I've done a lot of work here over the years. It was strange how I came to own it. I had no desire to own a home, especially one of

An orb captured on the way to Ruth's bedroom. It is near the location where I felt the burning on my left side.

this size. Being a single woman, what did I need with a house so large? When the last Horton died, a friend of mine took me here to see this place. She knew of my interest in architecture and, as you can see, this house has very lovely Victorian-era touches. As soon as I walked in, I had the strangest sensation. I felt as though I'd come home. After that, I couldn't stop thinking about this place. I know it sounds strange, but I felt as though it were calling to me. So, without thinking it through..." she said with a laugh, "I put down an offer and it was accepted. It's been thirty-five years and I haven't regretted my decision at all."

Steve smiled. "We've found in many of our investigations that a person will be drawn to a particular place to live because they're meant to do something there. In your case, you were meant to take care of this house and tell its story."

"I do believe you're right. Which is why I want very much to edit and publish the diaries I found. They're a fascinating look at life in the 1800s. It starts at the turn of the century and continues right up to the years following the Civil War. I'll get them so you can take a look."

On Fire

As Maggie left to retrieve the diaries, we finished our dessert and iced tea. I then leaned in towards Steve.

"What does it mean when you suddenly feel yourself on fire?"

"Knowing you, it probably means you're going to hell."

I made a face. "Cute." I then related the strange experience I'd had in the stairwell. Just as I was finishing, Maggie returned.

"What was that you said about a fire?" she asked.

I turned to find Maggie standing in the entranceway, her arms full of old journals, her eyes twinkling with interest. I repeated the details. Maggie listened quietly, then plopped the journals down in the nearest chair and turned swiftly on her heel.

"Show me exactly where you were standing," she commanded.

We got up from the table and walked out to the foyer. I re-enacted where I was standing. Maggie pointed and I turned to see that I was standing next to a photograph of an attractive dark-haired woman who appeared to be in her early thirties. She was dressed in the style of the 1940s.

"You're standing next to Ruth. She was a member of the Horton family and grew up here. I like to have photographs of the Horton family here on this table. I feel as though I'm honoring those before me who lived and loved this house." She bent over and picked up the photograph.

"Have you ever heard of the Cocoanut Grove Fire?" she asked. We shook our heads. "The Cocoanut Grove was a popular nightclub in Boston. It was the place to go in the thirties and early forties. Ruth and her husband, Albert, went to the Grove on November 28, 1942. While they were there, a curtain caught on fire which quickly spread. The club was filled beyond its capacity that night. You can imagine the reaction of the crowd when they realized there was a fire. Complete pandemonium broke out and there was a stampede to escape the burning rooms. This was in the day before fire codes, and the owner, wary of people buying drinks and not paying, was in the habit of locking the back doors. There was now only one way out and that was through a revolving door at the entrance of the club. In a frenzy to escape, people were crushed trying to get through those doors. The next day, the firemen found bodies piled atop each other, their bodies wedged against what was left of the doors. In the end, 492 people died, some from smoke inhalation, some from burning, many from being crushed." She glanced over at the picture of Ruth. "Sadly, it's believed Ruth and Albert burned to death."

A chill ran through me. "I must have felt her last moments in the fire," I whispered, shivering at the memory of the horrific pain.

It was distressing to look at the photograph of the vibrant young woman and not only know, but *feel* the way she'd so tragically died.

"Do you know which bedroom was Ruth's?" Amy asked.

"I believe it's the one to the left of the stairs, at the end of the corridor."

Still grief-stricken over my experience, I followed Amy and Lisa upstairs. Amy had a sense that Ruth was one of the spirits in the house and wanted to do some EVP work in her bedroom.

Recently, Maggie had begun to have difficulties climbing the steep set of stairs. She therefore lived on the ground floor, keeping the upstairs closed off. The rooms were empty of furniture and we had no trouble finding what had once been Ruth's bedroom.

The three of us sat cross-legged on the hard wood floor while Amy took out her recorder. After tagging the recording as to date, participants, and location, she began to ask her questions.

After a few minutes, Amy played back the tape. We sat stunned as we listened to the following:

> **Amy:** Bety felt your contact downstairs. She felt— (At this moment a hoarse screech is heard on the tape)
> **Amy:** How many spirits are in this house that wish to be cleared?
> **Response:** *Three*
> **Amy:** Is your husband here with you?
> **Response:** *Yes*[1]

"What do you think that screech was?" I asked after Amy turned the recorder off.

"There could be two reasons for that," Amy responded thoughtfully. "This is probably the first time in over sixty years that Ruth has actually spoken. She's not used to using energy to speak."

"And she died in a fire," Lisa added. "When Amy asked her first question, maybe Ruth was still feeling the effects of smoke inhalation."

We asked several more questions, but those were the only responses we received. We said a prayer for Ruth and Albert, then spent the rest of the day touring the barn and gardens. It wasn't until we were on our way home that we realized that in all the excitement of discovering Ruth's story and speaking with her, (as well as physically feeling her death), we'd completely forgotten the initial reason for our visit. We never did ask the spirits of the house if they minded Maggie transcribing their diaries.

Follow-Up

A follow-up visit is pending in order to help the three spirits who are stuck in Maggie's house to go Home and to discover if they agree to having the diaries transcribed and published.

---

[1] This EVP can be heard on our website: www.spiritlightnetwork.net

A Word About Spirit Guides

Whether you believe in the paranormal or not, everyone has spirit guides. Sometimes guides come in the form of animals. In shamanism, we call them our animal totems. If an animal appears to you three times in a short period of time, it's a safe bet that this is your animal totem. There are sites on the internet that will tell you what the animal represents. For example, wolf is about teaching. Turkey is about family. Eagle and hawk are about seeing the bigger picture. Squirrel signifies harvest – time to start gathering something into your life.

There are also spirit guides. Guides, whether animal or spiritual, come and go in your life depending on where you are on your life's path. Many people believe that deceased loved ones serve as guides. Sometimes they do. But – and this is very important – a guide cannot tell you what to do. They cannot interfere with your free will. They can guide and suggest and step in to save you in an emergency. But if you find yourself with a guide who is telling you what to do, when to do it, or if you find yourself with a psychic who is telling you the same thing, run the other way.

We humans are a stubborn lot. Sometimes we have to be hit over the head to learn a particular lesson. What we perceive as bad may not be bad in the long run. Sometimes we need to go through something tough in order to learn. Guides know that. They will step aside and allow you to go through something because they know you need to go through it. You can always talk to them and watch for signs that they are listening, whether it is a calmness that comes over you, or a slogan on a truck that suddenly makes sense. When I was going through a particularly bad patch in my life, I was walking through the streets of Boston thinking about my situation and how I could escape it. I thought about a particular co-worker who was making my life a living hell. I wondered what I could do to change it all. I happened to look up at that moment as a truck passed by and I saw on its side the words "Let it Go." I knew this was a gentle reminder from Guidance. I realized at that moment that I was making myself sick by worrying so much about a person whose actions I couldn't control. I did let it go and although she didn't change, I chose to change how I reacted to her. About two months later, I was able to leave that job, met Steve, and the rest, as they say, is history.

7

Something Wicked This Way Comes

I T WAS A GLORIOUS SUMMER DAY. I was sitting in my yard, enjoying the sight of the tiny chickadees and cardinals eating from my birdfeeder. I'd just hung up from Steve, who'd related a strange vision he'd just had. While mulling over his words, my cell rang again. Looking at the ID, I saw that it was Amy.

"Hey," I answered. "How are you?"

"I had the strangest dream last night. I had to call and share it with you."

Amy is blessed with the ability of receiving messages in the dreamtime. Many times they are directly related to an upcoming investigation. As it happened, the day before Steve had set up an investigation for that evening. He'd phoned me less than an hour before Amy and we'd shared some psychic impressions and visions we were already receiving about the investigation. I was naturally curious to hear what kind of dream Amy had experienced.

"I saw this large hole in the Earth and this dark being crawling out of it. I couldn't see its face, but it felt really creepy, like something demonic. It kept telling me I was worthless, that I didn't belong here. It kept pushing me to end it all now. Just as I felt myself believing him, it started to snow. As the snow settled on my face and shoulders, I instantly felt happy. At that moment, my kids showed up and we started throwing snowballs at this thing. We hit it in the back of the neck and when we did, it screamed. The weird thing is that I felt this grabbing pain in the base of *my* neck. He scrambled back into the hole, warning me that we were not done with each other yet."

I could physically feel Amy shiver over the phone.

"That is creepy," I agreed. "I talked to Steve this morning and he told me he's been having visions of something buried in the ground. While I was on the phone, I closed my eyes and saw this tall, Puritan-type figure standing in front of me. He reminded me of pictures I've seen of the Salem witch trial judges. Stern, with no compassion. And to top it off, the woman we're seeing tonight – Judi is her name – emailed Steve this morning and told him that as soon as she scheduled us to come over tonight, all hell broke loose in her house. Throughout the night, she kept hearing glass shattering and things crashing to the floor in her living room, but each time she went to investigate, nothing was out of place. She didn't get any sleep at all."

"Sounds like a winner. Can't wait."

We both laughed. "We are a sick crew, aren't we? Who else loves this sort of stuff?"

Oppressive Energy

At one time, Judi ran a successful yoga studio with a thriving clientele. Although her marriage had recently ended, she was eagerly looking forward to moving on with her life. Part of that involved buying a house on a quiet suburban street in a town located about a half hour north of Boston. It wasn't long after moving into her new home that Judi's life began to change.

But not in the way she'd expected.

Her yoga clients began to leave her with no explanation. She wasn't doing anything different; the only change was the new house, but they deserted her to the point that her business was in danger of folding, leaving her financially strapped. In the midst of this turmoil, she noticed her children emotionally withdrawing from her. Yet the worst was a dark foreboding energy that she couldn't shake, no matter how hard she tried. Naturally upbeat and gregarious by nature, she too began to withdraw from everything and everyone. This was putting everything in jeopardy, including her modest split-level house situated on a lovely acre and a half of land.

David, Joy, Amy, and Becky joined Steve and I on this investigation. Amy drove and we were chitchatting away when we were suddenly silenced as we pulled onto Judi's street. Our stomachs tightened, our chests ached and we found it difficult to breathe as the van filled with the presence of something sinister and threatening.

"What the hell is that?" Becky exclaimed as she rubbed her stomach with her hand.

I looked up the street towards our destination. "Whatever is at Judi's house is letting us know it's waiting for us."

We pulled into the driveway and piled out of the van. Becky immediately began snapping pictures on the well-manicured front lawn while I tried to get a handle on the increasingly oppressive energy that was weighing down on us.

Because of our ability to go into dark, menacing places without fear, we'd quickly become the "go-to" group for other paranormal teams who would rather leave the more terrifying hauntings to us. Judi had tried to use another group to investigate her home, but they had come away badly frightened. Convinced it was demonic forces haunting the house, they'd advised her to sell and get the hell out as quickly as she could. Financially unable to do that and frantic for help, she heard about us from a mutual friend and immediately called us in.

We rang the doorbell and it was soon opened by a tall, athletic woman in her early 40s, with a stylishly short haircut and a deep, husky voice. During introductions, I noted an intensity about her. She was obviously frightened by what was going on in her life, but she was also angry. As a successfully sharp businesswoman, she was accustomed to calling the shots, yet here was a situation she had no control over at all. Her energy was completely out of balance, snapping out in fury and frustration, and I found myself involuntarily stepping back.

She led us up a short flight of stairs. Climbing up, I glanced at Becky and Amy who mouthed the same word I was hearing in my own head – "alcoholism." I had no idea what it meant. Was Judi an alcoholic? Was the spirit that was haunting her an alcoholic? I had no choice but to wait and see if more information would come up during the evening.

Reaching the living room, Becky and Amy took off down the corridor towards the bedrooms to take pictures and do some EVP work. The rest of us gathered on the comfy red chairs and sofa. Balanced on the back of the couch was an adorable white Maltese who Judi introduced as Pippin. I immediately noticed that even the dog looked nervous and jumpy. Being a dog owner myself, I placed my hands on his trembling back and sent soothing healing energy to him. Joy joined me and we soon had the little animal resting comfortably.

"I just don't know what to do anymore and I'm really hoping you guys can help."

"We'll do our best," Steve said.

She explained about the strange downturn in her business, her hands slashing the air as she spoke. She was clearly agitated, but it became more pointed when she began to talk about the house itself. "Whenever I'm home, I feel depressed. It gets to a point where I don't want to go out. I don't want to do anything. I just want to hide. And that's not like me! I used to have tons of energy. I always had something going on. But the longer I stay in, the more difficult it is for me to get motivated to even move off the couch. I know this is going to sound crazy, but it's as if the house doesn't want me going out. Yet, when I do leave, and especially if I'm away for a couple of days, I'm fine. I'm back to my old self. It isn't until I return back here that I start getting that blah feeling again. Like I don't care about anyone or anything. At first, I thought it was just me. But my son, who recently went away to college, told me that when he came home, he started feeling this heavy energy around him, too. As a matter of fact, he's taken to spending nights at his friend's house. My daughter, who doesn't want to know anything about this stuff, is having trouble sleeping in her bed. She can sleep anywhere except in her own bed. Even poor Pippin here is not the same dog he used to be. He's always shaking and scared and he's suddenly developed all these stomach issues that have the vets baffled. My own stomach has been a complete mess since I moved in here. I'm barely eating as it is. Then there's the loud crashes at night. You would swear the living room is being completely trashed. But when I look, everything's fine." All of this was said in a rapid, staccato voice, as if she was afraid that if she stopped to breathe, she'd be prevented from getting the whole story out. When she finally did take a breath, I realized I had been holding mine!

"And finally, there's that *thing* in my bedroom. I don't know how else to describe it. It's a dark shadow that's pulled me out of my bed at night. And—" she hesitated, then forced herself to continue. "And it's touched me. Inappropriately." She looked up at us, the fear and anger visible in her eyes. "My life has been completely turned upside down. It's as if a dark cloud has descended over me and I don't know how to make it right again. This god-damned house is sucking me dry and that other paranormal group I called in did nothing! They told me the house was evil and I should get out. Where the hell am I going to go? I have no money, nothing! I'm barely holding on as it is. Just what the hell is in here?"

She was on the verge of losing her composure. Joy, David, Steve, and I quietly took on her hysteria, grounding it out through our feet. It didn't take long before we could see her visibly calming.

"How long have you lived here?" Steve asked.

"About three months. This house was supposed to be the start of a whole new life for me. My husband and I had just gotten a divorce and I wanted to get away from the bad memories the other house held. But this one certainly hasn't been any better."

She stared at each of us, her dark eyes snapping in frustration. "So what is going on? Do I have a demon here? Do I need an exorcism?"

Steve shook his head. "Not sure yet. We'll need to walk around and see what we pick up. Our group works by getting bits and pieces of the bigger picture. We have a saying – drama in life equals drama in death. Whatever is here is obviously very dramatic. We've learned never to go with the first impressions we get. We'll keep working through the layers, seeing what we each pick up, then we'll start putting it together until we get to the core reason why a place is haunted."

"I'm just curious, but do you know anything about the history of this house or the land?" I asked.

"This housing complex was built in the 1950s, but my daughter, who loves history, did find out that the land used to be owned by one of the Salem Witch Trial judges."

I got the familiar chill that told me I'd hit upon a truth of some sort. Judi's information confirmed why I'd seen the Puritan-like judge that morning. But how and why he figured in the present haunting remained to be seen.

Out of the corner of my eye, I saw Amy standing at the top of the stairs we'd just come up. She beckoned to me and I quickly excused myself, leaving Steve, Joy, and David to continue their conversation with Judi.

"What's up?" I asked.

"Check this out."

I followed Amy as she led me downstairs. Opposite the front door where we'd come in was the entrance to the basement. It was a large room, divided into two parts. The right side was your typical basement with storage boxes, sporting equipment and other items scattered about. The left side was set up as a bedroom, with pastel-colored wall paper, a dresser and a full-size bed with stuffed animals propped up against the pillows. It was very feminine and easy to guess this was where Judi's daughter slept. Amy directed me to one side of the bed while she took up the opposite side.

"Put your hand over the bed and tell me if you feel anything."

I leaned over where I imagined Judi's daughter would lie when she was asleep and put my hand out. I slowly waved it back and forth, wondering what I was supposed to find.

"I'm not feeling anything," I admitted as I continued feeling empty air.

"Reach higher."

I did as she instructed and just as I was about to tell her I still wasn't feeling anything, my hand suddenly felt engulfed in a ball of electrically charged energy.

I instantly yanked it back. "Holy cow!"

She nodded. "She's got an energy ball hanging over her bed."

This was the second time we'd come in contact with this particular phenomena. We ran about the room, waving our arms, looking idiotic to anyone who might see us as we tried to find any more energy balls or the source of this one. But there was nothing. Nor were there any abnormal readings on the EMF meter or the temperature gauge. We returned to the bed and once again put our hands into the mass.

The energy felt static and disruptive. It also felt very uncomfortable as it swirled around our hands and arms. We could only guess at what this unsettled energy was doing to Judi's daughter when she tried to sleep.

Amy describing the energy ball over Katy's bed.

We took pictures, then I quickly briefed Amy on what Judi had told us upstairs.

"No wonder her bedroom feels so creepy," Amy said. "When Becky and I went in to take pictures, it was – well, I'll wait for you to see what you get."

"Did you pick up anything yet on why we heard the word 'alcoholic'?"

Amy shook her head. "Not yet."

We ran upstairs and headed towards the back of the house.

Judi's bedroom faced out over the backyard, and at first glance, it was a cozy room with a queen-size bed and lovely forest green bedclothes. A large, intricately carved armoire stood in the far corner opposite the bed; on the wall hung calming and peaceful seascapes. Becky was leaning against the dresser, taking pictures as I came up.

I stood on the threshold and put out my spider sense. Strangely, I felt nothing.

"Is there something here?" I asked.

"Walk towards the bed," Amy suggested.

I shrugged and did as she asked. Suddenly, I caught my breath as a sharp pain – as if someone had grabbed my heart in their hand and crushed it – spread out throughout my chest. "Owww," I muttered, as I grabbed my chest and doubled over.

"This thing really doesn't like us being here, does it?" I gasped as I began the process of moving the energy through me.

"No it doesn't. When Becky and I stepped in here, we felt the same thing. What's strange is that as we moved around the room, the pain would come and go. I got the sense that it was attacking, then retreating, then attacking again. Whatever is in here is trying its best to frighten us so we'll leave."

That wasn't happening. On the contrary, it was making us more determined to get to the bottom of what was going on in Judi's house.

The pain subsided as I continued grounding. "Did you see what this thing looks like?" I asked.

She nodded. "It was the same black figure from my dream."

Charmed

The night air was refreshing and very welcoming after my experiences in Judi's house. By the time the group assembled outside, my breathing was normal and the pain was gone. We gathered around a large rectangular-shaped boulder that sat about twenty yards from Judi's back door. The moon was full and bright, adding a glow to our surroundings. David scrambled atop the rock and squatted down, placing his hands flat onto the cold stone.

Many people believe that rocks are inanimate objects, but as with plants and people, rocks also retain energy. David, who has spent years studying indigenous cultures and their relationship to the earth, shook his head from side to side. "That's interesting. The rock itself feels great, but there's something around it that feels off. Something's not right here."

"Really?" Judi asked. "One of the reasons I bought this house was because I was so drawn to that rock."

Amy, Becky, and I began to take pictures. We heard an exclamation from Becky a few moments later when she looked at the digital screen on her camera.

"Guys. You've got to see this." We gathered around her and were shocked to see a large, oddly-shaped mist materializing above the ground a few feet from where David was standing.

"What the hell is that?" I asked.

"That's amazing," Amy exclaimed. "That shape is exactly what I saw coming out of the ground in my dream."

She quickly looked through the pictures she'd just taken. "I can't believe this. I think I got the face of the dark entity that attacked me in my dream."

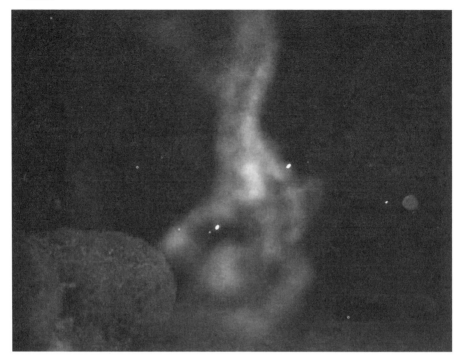

This image was captured behind Judi's house and matches the description of what Amy saw in her dream regarding a dark entity terrorizing Judi and her family.

It was difficult to see on her digital screen, but later that evening when we blew it up on Lisa's computer, we were stunned to see a face in one of the orbs Amy had captured.

Amy pensively looked back to the house. "There's a connection between this spot and Judi's house. I don't know what it is yet, but there's definitely a link between what's in the house and what's out here."

"I agree," Steve replied. "Remember that vision I had of something being buried in the ground? I think whatever is in that picture is warning us to keep away from it."

Judi stared at him in amazement. "How did you know I buried something near here?"

We looked at each other, hiding our excitement. Because of the nature of our work in fostering an understanding of the Other Side with the general public, especially families who may be in distress, we are not dramatic. We keep things relaxed and on an even keel. It keeps our clients calm and doesn't nourish any energies that may already be feeding on fear and drama. Since we were still gathering information, we didn't wish to add to Judi's emotional volatility.

However, this investigation was proving to be more melodramatic than we could have ever imagined. And as the next hour would prove, it would surpass expectations.

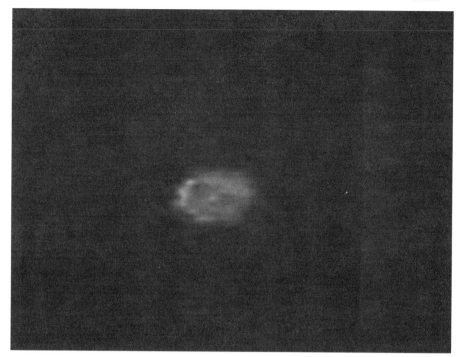

Is this the face of that dark entity?

"What did you bury?" Steve asked, his serene voice belying the interest I could see in his eyes.

"It was a gift from a woman my daughter used to work for. We'd had a falling out and as a peace offering, she gave me a money charm. She said that if I buried it in my backyard, it would bring me prosperity. I'd actually forgotten about it until you brought it up."

A foreboding fell over the group.

"When did you first bury this money charm?"

"Mmm, let me see. I think it was right after I moved in here. Since I viewed this house as the start of a new life, I didn't think it would hurt to have a bit of prosperity come my way as well."

Steve absently stroked his goatee. "Interesting. You buried it around the same time your life took a nose dive."

Judi's mouth dropped open as the realization hit her. "You don't think that charm has anything to do with what's going on here?"

"Anything's possible. What is this woman's name?"

A person's name holds their personal energy. Many times it is easy for us to connect to a person, regardless of time or distance, by connecting to the energy of their name.

"Her name is Laura Bocata."

A chill ran through the group. There was an ominous energy about Laura, a darkness that spoke of lies, deceit, and implacable anger.

"You had trouble with her, didn't you?" Joy asked.

Judi looked at her in surprise. "My daughter, Katy, started working in her little grocery store about six months ago. It wasn't supposed to be anything permanent. Just a little side job to make some extra pocket cash. At first, everything was great. Katy got along with Laura, thought she was wonderful. And Laura thought the world of Katy. She was kind and helpful and treated Katy as if she were her own daughter. I'm not sure when it started, but I began to notice little things that didn't feel right to me."

"Like what?"

Judi paused, not sure how to continue. She then heaved a heavy sigh. "The only way to describe it is to say that Laura began interfering in my relationship with Katy. It was as if she was trying to claim my daughter and take her away from me. At first, I thought I was just imagining things. You know how it is. And Katy liked her so much, I didn't want to interfere. But I quickly came to realize something was wrong. Katy became more withdrawn, more secretive. We'd always had a close relationship, but she became a person I didn't recognize anymore. I was so upset I drove straight to Laura's store and had it out with her. I made Katy quit right then and there."

"How was Katy after she quit?" Becky asked.

"Well, naturally she was angry with me. Accused me of interfering with her life and wouldn't speak to me for a few days. But, gradually, she became the Katy I knew. She wasn't moody or secretive anymore. A few weeks ago, in fact, she finally admitted to me that Laura was into the dark arts and had been teaching her how to practice it as well."

Another chill went through the group as the pieces started to fall into place.

"I can tell you that was no money charm," Steve said. "We need to try and find it."

She looked at him in bewilderment. "You honestly think that charm is responsible for everything?"

"Your life was fine until you buried the charm and had the falling out with Laura."

"But it was a little nothing charm. No big deal."

Steve told her about his vision and Amy's dream. "This indicates to me that Laura is a very powerful person. It's very easy for a person with that kind of power to put whatever intention they want into an object, no matter how small the object may be. The fact that she's placed a protection around the charm to make sure it isn't interfered with means she meant it to do you harm."

"This is too crazy," Judi replied.

"Everything was fine until you had the argument with Laura and buried the charm," Steve pointed out again. "And if it isn't the charm that's messing with you, we'll find out soon enough."

Judi shuddered. "Then let's dig the damned thing up." She looked around the yard, then clicked her tongue in disgust. "Crap. I don't exactly remember where I put it. I know it's near here though."

Steve turned to the group. "We'll just have to use our spider sense to find it. Shouldn't be too hard. It will have an extremely low vibration to it."

Steve turned on his heel and we began to slowly circle the area where Becky had captured the figure of the mist. After almost ten minutes, we still hadn't found anything. I was beginning to think it would be easier to find the proverbial needle in a haystack. We decided to expand the parameters of the search area on the off chance that the misty figure was trying to trick us. No sooner did we do that than Steve abruptly stopped. I looked up in time to see a visible tremor shake his body.

"It's right here," he declared. "It may not be in this exact spot, but it's very close."

We moved closer to where he was standing and sure enough, the telltale flare-up of pain in our chests and tightening in our stomachs confirmed that indeed, the charm was nearby.

"Wow. I feel like I want to throw up," Judi exclaimed as she came up behind us.

"There's a lot of Laura's will in the charm. Much of the dark arts is fueled by the practitioner's will. That's what you're feeling in your stomach area, which is why it hurts. She and that dark mist are imposing their will on you."

"Is that dark mist a demon?" Judi asked.

"Not really. There are lower vibrational entities that are used by people who practice the dark arts to do their bidding. If you've healed your fears and vulnerabilities, they have nothing to attach to and will leave you alone, no matter what the practitioner has done."

"A person can really do that?"

He nodded. "To have perfect balance, you need energy from above, called Heaven or whatever you want to call it, and below, which is the earth energy. Dark arts, though, don't use the celestial energy. They use earth energy. As I said earlier, it's very will-based. In other words, this woman's will was thwarted when you stepped in and took your daughter away from her. She, therefore, imposed her will on you to punish you for what you did. She called up a being that fed on all your vulnerabilities – your fears, your anger, your lack of control. The more things spun out of control, the more you reacted to it, giving it more of your energy to feed on. You then unwittingly anchored that energy here by burying the charm, thinking it was a prosperity charm, but which was obviously something else."

"So she basically cursed me."

"Yes and no. She did start the process, but you, not knowing what you were doing, fed it through your fears, your anger, etc. Believe me, I've dabbled in everything. You name it, I've tried it – witchcraft, wiccan, demonology, paganism. As crazy as it sounds, this stuff does happen."

"So what can we do to make it go away? Do we have to dig up the yard and find that damned charm?"

"I'll set an intention and see if that works. But before I do, I'd like to put a healing symbol in your stomach."

"Why my stomach?"

"Since you do yoga, you've heard of the chakra system, right?"

"Yes."

"Then you know that the human body has seven major points where we store energy. The third chakra, which is in your stomach area, rules the seat of willpower. Laura has basically been stealing your will and you, unwittingly, have helped in that process. By putting the healing symbol into your belly, it will take the intention of her will and transmute it, basically put light into her darkness. Does that make a little bit more sense?"

"It does."

Steve stepped to Judi's side and gently placing his hand on her stomach, he drew a healing symbol. There was a subtle shift in the air and Judi's eyes popped open in amazement.

"What did you just do? My stomach doesn't hurt anymore!"

"Laura was corded into you. I removed it."

"Okay, now what's that mean?"

"Remember you said that whenever you spend any time in your house, you feel as though the house is sucking you dry? Basically, that's exactly what was happening. Laura placed a cord in your energy field and like a vacuum, sucked up your energy. You also deal with the public. I'm sure you've had the experience of being with a person and when you walk away, you're completely drained." Judi nodded. "We call people like that energy vampires. You're getting corded by people who, whether consciously or subconsciously are feeding off your energy."

"So how do I stop this cording from occurring?"

"Don't react to people. Don't allow yourself to get sucked into their drama. You can remain energetically detached, but still be compassionate. The trick is not to leak your energy. The more you recognize how energy dynamics work between people, you'll actually get to a point where you'll feel when someone is trying to draw your energy away. Another little technique that may help is putting a physical barrier between you and the person. Take your thumb and middle finger and touch the tips together. You've created a circle. Now do the same with the other hand. Join the two circles and place this in front of your belly. You can do it in such a way that no one notices that you're actually putting up a barrier to prevent them from cording into you."

He asked us to get into a prayer circle. We joined hands and listened as Steve began to intone a Native American healing prayer. It wasn't long before I became aware of a cold prickle of energy blowing against the back of my neck. I shook it off and tried to concentrate on Steve's words, but the prickling persisted. It also grew colder although it was a warm June evening. My neck was now frigid. I turned my attention to this energy and felt a pair of eyes boring into the back of my head.

There is a shamanic technique called tracking that, among other things, allows the shaman to trace back the energy to its source. I began the tracking and quickly realized that, despite the distance and passage of time, Laura was still so corded into Judi and the charm that she knew exactly what we were doing.

Her face suddenly appeared before me, her oval face framed by long iron-grey hair, her blue eyes raging with anger over our audacity to dare interfere in her business.

A battle of wills began – her will intent on keeping the malevolence she'd unleashed on Judi intact – our wills intent on removing it.

It wasn't long before the black entity joined the fight. Its icy coldness jumped from person to person in the circle and I grimaced when I felt a searing jolt of pain on the back of my neck, as if a claw had imbedded itself into my skin. The back of the neck is considered the doorway to the soul and I could feel it literally attacking each one of us, looking for a vulnerability, something that would allow it to get in.

It swirled around us, its dense energy pounding against our backs as Steve continued the prayer. I felt myself being pushed and I saw that others in the group were trying to remain upright through the constant onslaught. We maintained our composure, throwing extra energy to Judi to keep her from caving in to the entity's desire to terrorize her. She was our weakest link. If she gave into the fear, it would only strengthen this entity.

To her credit, Judi remained steadfastly determined not to panic. Her decision to take back her life caused the entity to grow more frenzied. Denied the fear it had been feasting on, it redoubled its efforts to frighten us. It threw itself against us, chilling us to the bone. It flew up and down, to the right and to the left. It hit our backs and got right into our faces. Yet we remained calm. To give in now was to condemn Judi to an ever-downward spiraling existence. This was a challenge.

And we weren't giving in.

Then the prayer ended. We waited. The night grew still and quiet. After a few moments, a breeze blew up. It was soothing. And more importantly, it was warm.

We were no longer surrounded by icy air. The entity was gone. However, we still had Laura to deal with.

"She knows what we did and she is not happy," Steve said. "All during the prayer, she kept shoving her face in mine, shouting at me, threatening me for interfering." He looked to each of us. "Be prepared. She's probably going to come after us in the dreamtime."

"What about me?" Judi asked.

"I called upon our guides to watch over you. I've also energetically sealed your house from further attacks. I have a feeling that if she's going to come after anyone, it's going to be us."

"So you were able to break the curse?"

"For now." Judi's eyes widened. "We have one more thing to do. Amy had a dream about this thing climbing in and out of a hole in the earth. We need to find that vortex."

"What's a vortex?"

"Basically, it's a hole in the ground that contains highly charged energy. It's being used right now by this entity as a doorway to and from your house."

Judi looked around. "Is it in my backyard?"

"I don't think so," Amy said. "It felt like it's in your house."

"This just gets better and better," Judi moaned. "I ought to put a curse on her."

"NO!" we all shouted simultaneously.

"Magick given is magick owed, and payback's a bitch," Steve said. "You never want to owe anyone or anything. It's not worth it."

Starting back towards the house, Steve tried his best to allay Judi's concerns.

"Laura took advantage of your fears and anger. Each time you reacted to what was going on, you leaked your energy for this thing to feed on. It was obviously very good at amplifying your emotions. You over-react, you're pretty much breakfast, lunch, and dinner to this entity and others like him. Now that we've removed the cord, you need to start healing those parts of yourself so you don't get corded by Laura or anyone else."

"There's a lot there to heal," she admitted. "I've made some pretty bad choices in my life and lately they just seem to be coming back to bite me in the ass."

"The first thing to do is to stop looking at your choices as either good ones or bad ones. They were choices made in order to get you to step up and learn from them."

"Oh, I've learned from them! No more dysfunctional relationships with alcoholic men!"

Amy, Becky, and I exchanged knowing glances. So that was what the word "alcoholic" we'd heard meant.

"That's a start," Steve continued. "The more you recognize the lessons you've needed to learn, the more you can start to change that energy so you don't attract dysfunctional, alcoholic men to you anymore." He patted his stomach. "As I'm saying that, I can feel your belly tighten."

"It did! How did you know that?"

"Because I'm an empath. We all are in this group. I feel what you feel. You still have a lot of fears and anger stored up in your belly and by me saying what I did, it poked at a button. Which is actually a good thing. Now we can start looking at that button. When we get back inside, I'll do a healing on you while the group looks for the vortex."

The Vortex

As we re-entered the house, Amy and David were immediately drawn to the basement. While they went to check it out, Joy, Becky, and I searched the upstairs. Never having searched for a vortex, I wasn't sure what I was looking for. All I could do was pray that I'd know it when I found it.

I was scouting around the extra bedroom when I heard someone come up behind me. It was Amy.

"I think David and I found it. It's downstairs and wait until you feel this thing."

"You've got to be kidding."

As a paranormal investigator/psychic, I've had some very strange experiences, but this took top prize. I stared at David and Amy in disbelief.

"Wild, isn't it?" David said, smiling

Understatement of the year.

We were crouched around a spot on the basement floor nestled between the sporting equipment and storage boxes. Once again, I held my hand eye-level above the floor, just to make sure I wasn't dreaming.

Nope, I wasn't.

Although the concrete floor beneath my hand was ice cold, the air above it was blazing hot. We'd walked around the basement to see if other spots were warm. They weren't. We checked to see if there was a space heater, furnace, or vent that would give off this kind of heat in this one particular area. There wasn't. Only this spot, which measured about twelve inches by twelve inches, had hot pulsating air hovering over it.

"Wouldn't Judi have noticed something like this?" I asked.

"Take a look around. By the layer of dust on these boxes, I'd say the last time Judi was in this area was when she moved in," David answered. "And that was, what, about three months ago?"

"Now what? How do we close this thing?" Amy asked. We stared blankly at each other. Although each investigation adds to our body of knowledge, and we certainly don't claim to know everything, this was something completely new.

"I'll go upstairs and ask Steve what we should do," I said.

Steve has been a shaman for over thirty years. His vast experience dealing with every aspect of the Other Side has proven invaluable time and time again. If anyone would know how to close the vortex, it would be him.

I found him in the kitchen speaking with Judi, Joy, and Becky. After pulling him aside and telling him what we'd found, I listened quietly as he gave me instructions. I nodded, repeated back what he'd told me, then took off downstairs.

Amy and David looked up expectantly.

"We need to form a triangle over the vortex, hold hands and get our vibrations up as high as we can," I said. We did that, with Amy and David forming the right and left corners of the triangle and I at the top. We held hands and began the process of raising our vibrations to a point where our bodies were slightly shaking.

"What now?" Amy asked.

"I'm going to say a little prayer."

In the name of Creator, of the Christ, of the children of Mother Earth and of all those who have come before us, I ask that this vortex be sealed now and forever. Let this family find peace. Let this family find love. Let this family find healing. Let this family find You and the path You have set out for them. Allow the being that has used this doorway as an entryway return to whence it came. Know it is no longer wanted here. Know it will no longer be tolerated here. We ask that the Higher Consciousness of all that is assist us in closing this doorway now and forever. Amen.

"Amy, the snow in your dream was a metaphor for pure love and light. We need to pour that love and light down into the vortex, filling it up to the very top."

A light blazed in my mind's eye, growing brighter and brighter, enveloping the entrance to the vortex. Our bodies hummed, we swayed slightly back and forth from the powerful energy we were creating. We kept our concentration sharply focused on what we were doing.

I felt a sudden shift. The pulsating heat was retracting. Instead of coming out of the vortex, it was now moving backwards.

"Oh my God!" Amy exclaimed. "The energy's draining back down the hole."

"Now we seal it."

"How?"

"We put our healing symbols over the hole."

After several years of study, each of us were given shamanic rites – a ceremony that allowed us to access a higher level of energy. During the rite, we were given our own personal healing symbol that was attuned to our own personal energy. For anyone who has ever studied reiki, they will be familiar with healing symbols. They are a formalized intention to heal through the use of symbology.

We each leaned forward and drew in the air over the vortex our own personal healing symbol. We then held hands again, continuing to send love and light. In an instant, we all felt a shaft of white energy shudder through us, down through our feet, and into the floor. Although no sound was visibly made, I heard a roar in my ears.

Then all was still.

We opened our eyes and took a deep breath. Our faces were flushed. We shook out our limbs. It takes a lot of concentration to keep such a high vibration for any length of time.

David and Amy put their hands out over the spot and smiled.

"It's gone," Amy said.

"I don't feel anything either," David agreed.

I put my hand out. They were right. There was no heat. No pulsating energy. It was quiet. The air was cool, like the rest of the basement.

Amy hurried to the other side of the basement where Katy's bed was located. She put her hand in the air and felt along the length and width of her bed. "The energy ball is gone, too!" she exclaimed.

"Wow," I laughed. "No one is ever going to believe this."

A quote from Shakespeare filtered through my mind. "There are more things in heaven and earth than are dreamt of in your philosophy."

Wasn't that the truth?

We checked the rest of the house and immediately noticed the difference. The oppressiveness that had greeted us upon arrival was now gone. Each room, including Judi's bedroom, felt comfortable and cozy. Just like a home should be.

Follow-Up

Each of us were visited in the dreamtime by those things we fear most – loss of family members, loss of friends. In an especially vivid dream, I was hung upside down and clawed at. When I awoke, I found red marks on my wrists and shoulders. Yet out of the group, Steve suffered the most intense attacks. Because of his leadership role in breaking the curse, Laura threw everything in her arsenal at him, including a spirit that attached itself to him during the day, interfering with his energy and keeping him cold despite the warm weather. As with everything else in his life, he didn't react the way Laura expected him to. He and the rest of us maintained a detachment that eventually wore Laura down until she finally stopped.

Intrigued by the healings she'd received during our visit, Judi began to see Steve on a regular basis in order to work on the fears that had made her so vulnerable. She ceased being plagued by the oppression, apathy, and noises in the night that had made her life so unbearable. Her business improved, and about a year later, she sold the house and moved closer to her studio.

Why the Salem Witch Trial judge appeared to me remains a mystery. Maybe he was still checking up on his old property.

As for Pippin, our healing and Judi's changed attitude helped improve his own health and he's doing just fine.

Some Good Advice

We all get upset when someone does something to us that offends us or angers us. However, rather than get upset or offended, look at the situation as an opportunity to heal. If someone angers you, they have pushed a button within you. As crazy as it sounds, the person has actually done you a favor by showing you an aspect of your life that you need to heal. The trick now is to sit with your anger and figure out what is in YOU that allowed that button to be pressed. Try to trace it back to the original cause. For example, many people suffer from insecurity and struggle with their right to be here – to walk this earth as an equal human being. They feel unappreciated. Unworthy. Now, sit with that and try to figure out where those feelings came from. Was it from childhood? Was it a family member, a parent that made you feel worthless? Understand that everyone has a right to be here. Everyone has a path to follow. The more that you can work on that button, the more you can become whole. You'll know you've healed when the same situation arises and you don't feel the emotion you did before. You've removed the button. You can also begin to try and see why the other person did what they did. What was it about their childhood, their upbringing that makes them the way they are? Try to feel compassionate for the difficult path they've chosen for themselves.

Remember – it's all energy.

Cutting Cord Attachments

This happens quite often and can lead to illness, exhaustion, and loss of vitality, as witnessed by Judi. There are several types of cording; one of the most common is coming into contact with someone who literally drains you of your energy. I'm sure most of you reading these words have experienced this at one time or another. You meet someone, you speak for a few minutes, and when you turn away, you suddenly find yourself exhausted. Or you have a friend who constantly uses you as a sounding board for all their problems. They feel great after your talk; you feel like a wet dishrag. Guess what? They've corded into you and have taken your energy.

So someone has corded into you. What do you do?

The first thing you do is try and find a quiet space. State your intention (either silently or out loud) that you wish to remove any and all cords from anyone who doesn't serve you. The reason you state the intention in this manner is that you may not want to remove cords from your husband/wife or children. Next, rub your hands together. With your dominant hand, gently scan your abdomen area. When I do this, I will feel what appears to be a cold spot above the area where the cord is. You may feel a tingling in your hand. Just know that the energy will feel a little different. Sometimes when you're doing this, when you hit the area where the cord is, you may actually see a face, get a name or get a sense of the person who has corded into you. With your dominant hand, pull the cord out and picture white light closing up the area where the cord was attached.

Something to keep in mind with cording is that if you come back in contact with the person whose cord you removed and allow yourself to get sucked back into their drama, or you find yourself thinking and dwelling over them, the cord will instantly reconnect itself.

No one should be feeding off your energy. Everyone should be getting their energy from the Higher God Source.

Also, if people feed off the living while they are alive, there is a high probability they will continue to feed off the living when they die. This is called a spirit attachment and is addressed in another chapter.

8

I Want My Head Back

NOT ALL OF OUR INVESTIGATIONS ARE FRIGHTENING. Some are benign, some are poignant, and some seek us out when we're off doing other things. Each experience teaches us more about why spirits remain stuck. Sadly, some of the reasons the dead don't move on are indicative of the strange things we humans cling to for what we believe is necessary for our happiness – both on this side and the other side of the Veil.

The following story took place in the autumn of 2006. There was a special excitement within the group. We'd been invited to speak at Contact II, a paranormal conference hosted jointly by the Berkshire Paranormal Group and the New England Ghost Project. The conference was being held in North Adams, Massachusetts at the Houghton Mansion, a haunted location that has been featured many times on television and in books. There were several speakers from all over New England speaking on subjects ranging from the art of capturing EVPs to the lore surrounding vampires. We were scheduled to do two presentations, one on shamanism and the other on our adventures as the team that, as our slogan says, "We tread where others dread."

North Adams is located in the northwestern part of the state, bordering on the state of Vermont. Steve, Joy, David, and I drove the two and a half hours down Route 2 that runs parallel through the center of Massachusetts and which, in centuries past, was the main thoroughfare for the Mohawk Indians. The conference was due to start that Friday evening and we were running late. Luck was with us. We weren't scheduled to speak until the next day, so we were spared having to speed down Route 2 to make it on time.

We quickly checked into our hotel and set off to find the Houghton Mansion. After a few wrong turns, we found ourselves coming down a very steep hill. At the bottom and to the right was a grassy lot which was filled with cars. We guessed this was the mansion, especially when we turned right and saw an extravagantly large white and blue house, behind which was an incongruous brick addition that clearly did not belong to the original architecture. We knew that the mansion had been built in the 1890s by North Adams' first mayor, Albert Charles

The exterior of the very haunted Houghton Mansion located in North Adams, MA.

Houghton. In 1926, the mansion was bought by the Masons and a large Masonic Temple was erected where the formal gardens had once stood.

We eagerly entered and immediately saw why the Berkshire Paranormal Group, who is made up of several Masons, organizes the different paranormal conferences and ghost hunts. The mansion was in much need of repair and renovations, the odor of damp mildew surrounding us as we came into the foyer. Their events raise money to keep their lodge and the historical building from deteriorating further.

To the left of the foyer was Mr. Houghton's study. The walls were a rich dark wood reminiscent of the Victorian era, as was the period furniture. To the right was what had once been a large living room, and beyond that, doors that led to an enormous ballroom. It was in the ballroom where chairs were set up for the audience to listen to the various speakers. At night, the chairs would be pushed into a circle for the traditional midnight séance held during the conferences and their annual Halloween ghost hunts.

We were met at the door by Josh Mantello, co-founder and lead investigator for the Berkshire Paranormal Group. He had on his black T-shirt and baseball cap which featured a Triangle enclosing a seeing eye which is the logo for their group.

"Hey, glad you guys could make it," he said as he shook all our hands. "Great news. Both your talks are sold out."

"Awesome!" Steve said. "Sorry we're late. Have we missed anything?"

"Nah, not really. I did my introductions, talked you guys up really big. We had two speakers, who went over well. Right now one of our team members is leading a group over to the cemetery to see where the Houghtons are buried. If you want to go, I can take you over there."

I smiled. "Nothing like a cemetery at night."

"I'm parked out front. You can follow me over."

Hillside Cemetery

Founded in 1791, Hillside Cemetery houses the graves of a troop of Civil War soldiers, an eyewitness to Lincoln's Gettysburg Address, and, of interest to us, the burial site for the Houghton family.

The cemetery wasn't far from the mansion, so we all climbed into our van and followed Josh as he zipped through the streets of downtown North Adams. In no time at all, we were pulling into a very dark and spooky cemetery. In the distance, the night lights of North Adams twinkled. However, in the cemetery itself, I could barely see my hand in front of my face. Naturally, being the great ghost hunters that we were, none of us had thought to bring a flashlight. Thankfully, Josh had the forethought to be well prepared, so we huddled behind him as he led us among the gravestones towards the section where the Houghton family was buried.

There was already a small crowd gathered around the above-ground graves of Mr. A.E. Houghton and his family. We listened as Greg Onorato, another member of the Berkshire Paranormal Group, told the sad story of the Houghton family.

At the turn of the century, Mr. Houghton was the mayor of North Adams. He was also the owner of one of the first cars to be seen in North Adams. In the spring of 1914, that idyllic time before the horrors of World War I would scorch Europe, he and his family decided to take a drive. This was before asphalt highways and paved streets. While trying to maneuver around a soft bend in the road, the chauffeur, John Widders, lost control in the loose dirt and the car went down a steep embankment. It rolled over three times, badly injuring Mr. Houghton and killing his daughter, Mary. Devastated by the accident for which he blamed himself, Widders shot himself the next day in the barn behind the mansion. A week later, Mr. Houghton died of a heart attack, brought on, some say, by the trauma of losing his beloved daughter and the suicide of his chauffeur. Since then, the mansion has been purportedly haunted by the spirits of Mr. Houghton, Mary, and John Widders.

Standing in the cool evening air, we didn't feel any energy around the Houghton gravesite, which wasn't surprising. It's been said that, contrary to popular belief, graveyards are generally not haunted. Apparently, ghosts would rather hang out in places they loved rather than where their bodies ended up.

"There's another spot I want to show you guys," Josh said. "I want to test to see how good your psychic abilities are."

I inwardly groaned. To be honest, I hate when people do this to me. I'm not a performing seal and when I have to "prove" myself, I actually get too nervous to be able to get anything. However, Josh was a friend and instead of taking offense, we all looked forward to the challenge. He led us down a small hill and, careful to keep within sight of his bobbing flashlight, I gingerly jumped over the gravesites in the dark. I know it's crazy, but I'm always a little uncomfortable walking over burial sites. I feel as though I'm walking on someone's body, even if they are six feet down.

"Before we get to the spot I want to show you, check this out!" Josh exclaimed as he came to a stop before a simple headstone. We gathered around and immediately noticed that overlooking the headstone was a small statue of the Virgin Mary. It would have been tranquil except for the fact that the Virgin's head was missing.

"We've had some trouble with vandalism and someone stole her head," Josh explained. "Cut it clear off."

As he said that, I felt a surge of energy and a tightening of my stomach, indicating the presence of a spirit with a strong will. I glanced at each of my companions, but there was no indication on their faces that they were feeling what I was feeling.

"Kids like to dare each other to come up here late at night. The headless statue creeps them out and it's a kind of an initiation if they can stay out here alone for a night."

"Do you know who took the head?" I asked, saddened to see the desecration of such a pretty statue, not to mention the disrespect shown to the deceased over whose grave the Virgin had once graced.

"Unfortunately, no."

The anger continued to build. Before I realized what was happening, I saw in my mind's eye a bedroom and a teenage boy sitting on his bed. I was puzzled at first by what I was seeing. Then, in an instant, I saw the Virgin's head in the corner of his room, hidden under discarded clothes. I caught my breath.

I was seeing where the head was and the boy who had taken it!

However, I had no proof, no name, nothing. Just an image playing in my head. Along with the sudden shrill of a woman's voice ringing in my ear.

"Get me my head back! I want my head back!"

Surely the others were hearing this? But as I looked to each of them, I saw Steve engaged in conversation with Josh, while Joy and David were standing a short distance away checking out some of the other gravestones in the feeble light of Josh's flashlight.

From reasons known only to her, the woman had attached herself to me and was pushing me to find this boy's house and retrieve the statue's head.

Lucky me.

"I'm sorry, but I can't get the head back," I tried to explain in a conversation taking place silently in my head. "I don't even know where that kid lives or if he still has it. Besides, I'm just here for the weekend—"

"I don't care! I want my head back!" she screeched at me.

"Suppose I did find him. What am I supposed to do? Knock on his door and say, "Hey, I just happened to be talking to the ghost who owns the head you stole and she wants it back. That would go over well, wouldn't it?"

"I want my head back! I want my head back!"

Her parrot-like chant was interrupted when Josh came up and pointed off into the darkness.

"Let me take you to that place I was talking about earlier."

The group started out and I was bringing up the rear when the woman's once again hammered against my ears. "Where are you going? You've got to get my head back! I want it now!"

I sighed. This was getting to be a scene right out of the movie *Ghost*, with me playing the Whoopie Goldberg role. This screeching woman was taking over my thoughts and I wasn't happy about it.

This is an occupational hazard for those who are sensitive to the Other Side – especially in dealing with those who haven't crossed and remain stuck in their drama. They demand to be heard and, many times, demand action on your part. They cling to things that, in the long run, don't matter anymore. I tried to explain this to her, but she was having none of it. Her will was strong and she was determined to have me get the head back for her. I slowed down my step and turned all my attention to her.

"Look lady, you've got to stop bothering me. I can't do anything about it. I wish I could, but I can't. Now go away!"

"But—"

"I mean it! GO AWAY!"

Hadn't this woman ever heard of free will?

I felt her energy again, but managed to forcefully shove it away. I hurried along and caught up with the group as we came over a slight hill.

"You hear that?" Joy asked as I came up alongside her.

At first I was happy that she was hearing the woman as well. Maybe she could deal with her better than I could. But it wasn't the woman's voice that filtered through my mind as we approached an expanse of treeless lawn. It was the distinct sound of young voices.

A few yards ahead of us, we saw Steve turn to Josh. "There are children buried here," he said as we heard the ghostly sounds of children laughing and playing, though the graveyard itself remained silent in the dark stillness of the night.

"That's right," Josh exclaimed. "This is the section of the graveyard where the children are buried."

He pointed his flashlight to a spot in front of us, illuminating a row of about ten small gravestones that had been impossible to see in the dark.

We slowly walked along the tiny stones, sadly reading the names of children who had died much too young. The saddest was a family buried together who had lost six babies in stillbirth.

"I think we ought to do a circle and see if we can get any of the children to go Home," Steve replied.

"What do I have to do?" Josh asked, never having taken part in spirit releasement.

"You'll need to get your vibration as high as you can," Steve explained. He placed his hand on Josh's chest and opened up his heart chakra with a combination of prayer and energy work.

We held hands and listened as Steve called on the angels and guides and parents of the children to come and lead them to a happier place. He calmed any fears the children may have had about leaving, but there were a few who were too afraid to leave a place where they felt safe. And without the whole group leaving, none of the children would leave the others. After another prayer, we did manage to get a small number of children to go to the Light, but the majority still preferred to stay. We closed the circle by telling them that we respected their decision and that, when they were ready, they could leave any time they wanted. By this time, the night had grown considerably chillier and I, for one, was eager to get back to our warm hotel room.

"Do you ever force spirits to leave?" Josh asked when we were done.

Steve shook his head. "We respect their free will. We only become insistent when they are actively interfering with the living. What we do is offer them a choice. You see, right now, they don't know they have a choice. They are stuck and unable to see the Light. What we just did gave them the opportunity to see that Light. To feel the love and peace from the place we call Home.

Now they have a choice to stay or move on to that higher place of existence."

We retraced our steps and as we drew nearer to the headless statue, the energy once again increased dramatically. Excited to see we'd returned, I heard the woman begging for help to find the head of her statue. Before I could say anything, Steve, picking up on the same energy, slowed his step. "I think we need to do something for the woman whose gravesite was desecrated."

"You think?" I remarked, a headache starting to form behind my eyes from her incessant yelling.

"What do you mean?" Josh asked.

"She won't leave until the head is returned to the statue," I explained, the yelling growing painfully louder in my head.

"The town tried to replace the head, but it was stolen a second time. All I know about her is that she was very religious and spent years saving her money to have that statue look over her final resting place."

By this time Joy had tuned into the woman's energy and I could see her rubbing her temples as if to ease the pounding that she too was feeling.

"She's very angry," Joy replied. "She's insisting the head be replaced."

"Not much we can do about that. I doubt the town will pay to replace the head a third time," Josh explained, sympathetically staring down at the woman's grave.

"What about her family?"

Josh shrugged, but said nothing.

"Maybe we can all tell her that it doesn't matter whether the head is returned or not," I ventured. "What's important is that she continue her journey Home. I know the head is a reflection of her religious belief, but ultimately, it's just a material thing. She's putting way too much energy into a piece of stone."

Steve put his hands out and we formed a circle. For the second time that evening, Steve intoned a prayer of understanding, of forgiveness of what had been done to her grave and that, regrettable as the desecration of the statue was, there was a place where she could find the peace and tranquility that she obviously hadn't found yet.

Yet, no matter how convincing Steve was, the woman refused to budge. Once again, my mind was bombarded with visions of the teenager's bedroom and the stolen head.

"I don't think it's working," I muttered, my hands and feet growing colder by the minute. "She just won't go without her head."

Just as we were about to give up, Joy exclaimed, "I know what we can do. She obviously had a strong connection to Mother Mary. Why don't we try reciting the Hail Mary? That might help."

At this point, we were willing to try anything. We closed our eyes and together, we recited the Hail Mary, followed by the Our Father. Sure enough, as the words were spoken, I felt her energy growing lighter and lighter.

Regardless of what religion you may follow, prayers hold very powerful energy. Try reciting your favorite prayer slowly, *feeling* the energy of each and every word as you say them. Open your heart and mind as you do this. Hopefully you'll experience a tingle or a surge of energy surrounding you as you speak the prayer.

We all felt a shift of energy as a powerful force stepped into the circle. I knew at that moment that a powerful Guide had come to help the woman Home. In my mind's eye, I saw this being of pure white light reach out and take her hand and, as happens when I'm performing a clearing, I felt my energy rise and accompany them to the Doorway. I watched as she and the Guide stepped through the door and I felt my body shudder, telling me that she was finally Home. I opened my eyes and by the expressions on my team's faces, I knew they had also felt her go.

"Wow, that was amazing," Josh said, his face in awe at what he had just experienced.

"That was a great idea, Joy," Steve said. "Obviously any other kind of prayer wasn't going to work. She needed to hear what she was familiar with."

"What do you mean?" Josh asked.

"If you're dealing with a Native American spirit, saying a Christian prayer isn't going to help. Or, for example, coming across the spirit of a Protestant and saying a Catholic prayer. Or the presence of a colonial and saying an Indian prayer. You need to say something that they're going to recognize and be familiar with in order for them to understand what's happened. As a religious woman who loved Mother Mary, it was appropriate to recite the Hail Mary."

Walking back to our van, I took a deep breath, grateful for the soothing quiet running through my head. "Quick thinking, Joy. You saved us from doing a door-to-door search throughout North Adams to find Mother Mary's head."

She gave me a pointed look. "What do you mean 'us'?"

Raising Your Vibration

Here is a quick way to raise your vibration. The human body has seven major chakras (or energy centers). The first is located at the base of the spine, the second below the belly button, the third above the belly button, the fourth in the heart area, the fifth in the throat, the sixth on your brow, and the seventh on the crown or top of your head. Starting with the first, imagine a ray of white light bathing each chakra (which is shaped like a round disk). Continue up each chakra until you reach the 7th, which is on the top of your head. You may feel tingling in each chakra as you cleanse it. However, there are five other chakras located above your head. Try to see five round disks above your head and infuse each one with radiant white light. As you're traveling up each of these chakras, you should feel yourself getting lighter and lighter. You may feel yourself tingling. That's good. That means your vibration is rising as you go up each chakra. Keep in mind, however, this is a quick and easy way to raise your vibration. In order to *keep* your vibration high, you need to heal any issues that may reside in any particular chakra.

9

Remember the Boys

A LMOST EVERY NEW ENGLAND TOWN has what's called a Common – a small plot of land usually located in the center of town where, in the early days, the meetinghouses and churches were built and where, during the Revolutionary War, the local militias held their musters. The meetinghouses are almost all gone, as are the soldiers, but the "commonly held" ground is still there. This was, and remains, the heart of the village where, to this day, several roads converge like the spokes of a wheel.

Near such a common in one of those quaint New England towns, an old house stands that, like many such dated houses, has seen many transformations in its long history. Once a farmhouse, then a business establishment, followed by a time as a boarding house, the white clapboard building is now home to three apartments.

On the second floor lived a young family of three – father, mother, and a young daughter. They'd lived in their apartment for a few months, and from the beginning, they'd been plagued by the sounds of running, doors slamming, and the unmistakable sensation of being watched. One morning, the young mother Kirsten was at the stove making breakfast when she had such a frightening experience that she was ready to move out right then and there.

Soon after, Kirsten became aware of a new friend in her four-year-old daughter, Hannah's, life. The child consistently spoke of a little boy who liked to stay inside the large plastic playhouse that her parents had erected in her playroom. He was shy, Hannah told her, and didn't trust people very much. This went on for a few weeks and Kirsten chalked the little boy up as a figment of Hannah's active imagination. However, she began to rethink her position when things turned darker. She noticed Hannah playing on the other side of the small room, as far away from the playhouse as she could get. At first, Hannah refused to tell her why. She simply stopped approaching the playhouse and soon, she stopped going into the room unless Kirsten accompanied her. After a few weeks of gentle questioning, Hannah finally admitted that the little boy wouldn't let her in the playhouse. If she tried, he would turn mean and tell her, in no uncertain terms, that he wanted to be left alone.

In the midst of this, Kirsten's husband, Jonah, suddenly began to experience sharp pains in his left arm. He visited the doctor numerous times, but they could find nothing. The pain steadily increased to a point where it was extremely difficult for him to move his arm. What puzzled Jonah was the inconsistency of the pain. Sometimes it was so bad, he couldn't move his arm at all. Other times, it was as if the soreness had never existed. He never knew when it would hit and it became frustrating as he struggled to go about his life and job without the debilitating pain.

Jonah and Kirsten came to our attention through their acquaintance with Amy and Becky. The two sisters heard their story and decided to do a preliminary investigation on their own.

They did a walkthrough of the apartment and quickly focused on the energy in Hannah's playroom. Becky took a series of photos and captured the image of a small boy in overalls standing in the window.

This was confirmation that Hannah's playmate was real. They attempted to communicate with the boy. At first shy, he refused to talk and remained hidden in the playhouse. Calling on their experience as mothers of small boys, Amy and Becky were able to persuade the little boy to come out of his hiding place. By this time,

Is this image of the little boy wearing old-fashioned overalls who fell to his death from this window over 100 years ago?

Amy had begun to occasionally use a pendulum in her attempt to communicate with spirits, a technique borrowed from Maureen Wood, psychic for the New England Ghost Project. The pendulum is used, not because we need this to communicate with spirits, but more as a visual tool for the clients to actually see communication taking place. The pendulum will move in certain directions in answer to a *yes* or *no* question. In Amy's case, a swing counterclockwise meant *yes*. A swing clockwise meant *no*. No movement at all meant there would be no answer.

Using the pendulum, Amy and Becky were able to discover that the boy had lived in the house in the early 1800s when it was a farmhouse. Hannah's playroom had been his room and he'd died at the age of ten by falling out the window to the hard packed dirt below – the same window where Becky captured his image.

Throughout the rest of the apartment, they picked up on the energy of several other spirits. Overwhelmed by what they were finding, they decided to call in the rest of the team.

A Multitude of Ghosts

It was a cool late summer evening when we arrived at the house. On this investigation, the team was made up of Steve, Lisa, Joy, Becky, Amy and me.

The moon was full, sending shadows across the front porch. I paused on the threshold and looked out over the surrounding streets, trying to picture in my mind's eye what this must have looked like a hundred years before – rows and rows of corn and crops where now stood suburban housing and concrete streets.

I turned to follow the team up a narrow flight of stairs to the second floor where we were met by Kirsten and Jonah. They were a young couple in their mid-twenties. Kirsten was medium height, thin with dark hair. Jonah stood about five-foot-nine inches, muscular with a military-type blonde buzz cut. Their daughter, Hannah, was an adorable little girl with Shirley Temple-type blonde curls. Although it was around 7:30 at night when we arrived, she was still full of energy, running around the apartment with toys in tow.

Entering the small foyer, we noted that the kitchen was immediately to our left. The living room was to our right and through the living room was the master bedroom where all three slept. To the left of the living room was a small corridor that opened out to Hannah's playroom and the bathroom.

We gathered in the living room and quickly became aware of the presence of a multitude of spirits, both male and female. We decided to say nothing yet until we could gather more information.

Jonah played quietly with Hannah as Kirsten launched into her story.

"It wasn't too long after we moved in that we began to hear footsteps walking from the living room into our bedroom. This would happen at all times of the day and night. They sounded like men's boots because they were so heavy. Hannah then started telling us about a little boy who would come and play with her in her playhouse. At first we thought it was just an imaginary friend. But then we actually heard a little boy laughing. When we went into the room, there was just Hannah."

"Tell them about your experience in the kitchen," Becky prompted.

"That was bizarre. I've always had the feeling when I'm in the kitchen of being watched. No matter what I do, or what time of day or night it is, I just can't get rid of the feeling that someone is watching me. A few weeks ago, I was at the stove, making breakfast when I felt someone come up behind me. I thought it was Jonah. I was therefore shocked when a woman's voice said, 'You're doing that wrong.' Totally freaked me out. You have no idea how hard it was for me to finish frying up the egg before I could get the hell out of there."

"Anything else going on?" Steve asked.

"A few times we've heard what sounds like a group of people talking in the living room. When we check it out, there's nothing there. At first we thought we were just imagining things. But when we talked to our neighbors upstairs, turns out they've been hearing footsteps and weird noises in their apartment as well."

As Kirsten went through the litany of experiences, Jonah had remained quiet. It wasn't until she was done that he began to tell us of his own experiences.

"It was a few weeks after we moved in that I saw a face in the bathroom mirror. It was in the morning and I was getting ready for work. I was shaving and I looked up and saw this old man looking at me. Now, I was in the Marines. There's nothing that scares me. But that was unnerving. It wasn't too long after that I began experiencing pain in my left arm. It comes and goes and doctors can't explain what's going on."

"Where exactly does it hurt?" Steve asked.

"My entire arm, from my shoulder down to the tips of my fingers. Sometimes it's excruciating, sometimes it's fine with no pain at all. It's frustrating because I never know when it's going to hit."

"Do you mind if we walk around?" I asked.

"No, go right ahead."

A Happy Reunion

I pulled Becky aside. "Do you want to show me the room where you took the picture of the little boy?"

She nodded and led the way through the living room, down to the end of the corridor.

The room was small, with Hannah's toys strewn about the floor. A pink plastic playhouse was standing against the wall. Next to the playhouse were two picture windows that looked out over a parking lot. Becky pointed to the left window. "That's where I got the photo of the boy."

We walked further into the room and stood in the center, trying to pick up on the energy of the boy. We both had the strong sense that he was hiding. It made sense. He didn't know us, we were adults and it was obvious he felt more comfortable with Hannah than he did with us.

At that moment Amy entered.

"The little boy is around, but he's hiding," I explained.

"Last time we were here, I got the sense that he's very lonely," Becky replied.

"I'm not surprised," I responded. "Everyone he ever knew has been long gone."

"I really felt that he was missing his mother."

"Maybe we can reunite them."

"Can you do that?" she asked.

"We can try."

The three of us held hands and began the process of raising our vibration as high as we could. I always equate this process to having one foot in the material world and one foot in the spiritual world.

In a situation such as this, we use our energies to try and bring the two planes of existence – the plane of existence the boy's mother is on and the plane of existence the boy is on – close together so they can see each other. It takes a great deal of concentration and help from our own spirit guides. We said a little prayer to set the intention and waited as our energies adjusted to allow the mother to come forward. After five minutes, we felt a lighter, loving energy enter the room. We instinctively knew this was the boy's mother and asked her to enter our little circle. We then asked the little boy to come forward. It took a bit of cajoling to convince him to leave his hiding place, but as he drew closer to us, he began to see his mother standing with us. He flew forward into our circle and into her arms and we were enveloped in a loving, emotional energy as they were reunited after almost a century of being apart. We watched as she took his hand and led him away to the place where he wouldn't be lonely or frightened anymore.

"Oh my God," Becky remarked as she wiped a tear away. "That was so beautiful." As a mother of four, she identified fully with the mother and deeply felt their reunion.

Amy and I took a deep breath, taking a moment to allow our bodies to re-acclimate themselves back to the material world. We then quickly went through the rest of the apartment, taking pictures and doing mini-EVP sessions before ending up back in the living room.

Breakfast Anyone?

"Why don't you show us where the woman spoke to you?" Steve asked Kirsten. She led us all to the small kitchen. The stove was to the right of the entrance, and a small dinette set was set up against the far wall. I sat down on one of the chairs while Steve leaned against the wall next to me. Kirsten went up to the stove and Jonah hung back by the refrigerator.

"I was standing here when I felt someone come up behind me," Kirsten said. "I've felt that presence a lot when I'm in here. But that morning was the first time she spoke to me. She leaned over my shoulder and whispered, 'You're not doing it right.'"

"She didn't like the way you were making breakfast?" Lisa asked.

"Apparently. I was just frying up some eggs and bacon and I guess she didn't like the way I was doing it."

"Thank God she doesn't live in my house," I retorted. "Being the world's worst cook, she'd absolutely hate me!"

Acknowledging her presence caused the spirit to make an appearance. The room suddenly became colder and Kirsten shivered.

"She's here, isn't she?" she asked as the goosebumps erupted up and down her arms.

"I'd say so," Steve asked. He fell silent for a moment. "There seems to be a number of people here. Men and women of all ages." He looked up and met Kirsten's eyes. "Do you know anything about the history of this place?"

"A little."

"Do you know if this was a boarding house at one time?"

Jonah gasped. "How did you know?"

Steve smiled. "It feels to me that this woman was the cook for the boarding house which is why she's in this particular room all the time. That explains why she'd criticize the way you were cooking. She was very particular in life and continues to be that way in death."

A surge of strong-willed energy flew through the room. "She still thinks this is her kitchen," Joy remarked.

Steve nodded. "Exactly."

While Kirsten and Jonah digested our discovery, we felt another energy come into the room. This one was an older male. His presence brought up a great deal of sadness and guilt and I had to catch my breath as it overwhelmed me. As he moved into the room, Jonah suddenly yelped.

"Damn it, there goes my arm again." He tried flexing his hand, but he winced in pain.

I felt the man draw closer to me and before I could stop myself, I blurted out, "Anzio."

"What's that?" Steve asked.

"I just heard the word Anzio pop into my head."

"What is an Anzio?"

"It was a World War II battle fought in Italy late in the war. It led to the allies taking the city of Rome. A lot of Americans fought in that battle."

A chill ran through me, telling me that I was accurately perceiving what the spirit was trying to tell me. Once again, a name popped into my head. Usually, I'm not that good at getting names. But this one was so crystal clear, I decided to go with it. "He says his name is Richardson. He's upset because no one remembers or cares about the sacrifices he and his friends made. He lost a lot of comrades during that battle and no one even remembers it today." An image started to form in my mind's eye and I saw an older gentleman, about five-foot-eight inches tall. What shocked me was that he was missing his left arm. Steve and I exchanged glances; he'd seen the man too.

"Jonah, you said you were in the service, right?"

"Yes, I was. Marine sergeant."

"And it's your left arm's that's in pain?"

"That's right."

"Oh, wow," I muttered under my breath.

Jonah looked at us suspiciously. "Why are you asking?"

"I think we figured out what's going on with your arm," Steve replied. "Have you ever heard of like energy attracting like energy?"

Jonah shook his head. "Not really."

"This gentleman – Richardson – was a soldier. If what Bety is getting is correct, he fought at the Battle of Anzio. Since this was a boarding house at one time, I'll bet he lived here. You were a soldier. He was a soldier. That's the energy he knows and recognizes, which is why he's been hanging around you. I can see him standing in front of me plain as day." Steve leaned forward. "He's missing his left arm. The same arm you've been feeling pain in."

"But why would I feel pain if his arm is gone?"

"Many times when people lose a limb, they continue to feel what we call phantom pain," Amy explained, using her background as a nurse to explain the situation to Jonah. "Even though the arm or the leg is gone, they still feel pain where the limb would have been."

"And you think I've been feeling Richardson's phantom pain?" Jonah asked.

"Yes, we do."

He shook his head, not sure what to make of what we'd just told him. We decided to do a circle to see if we could help Richardson and the other spirits who inhabited the house move on. Steve led the prayer. When we were done, we put out energetic feelers.

"I can't believe it," Jonah exclaimed. "The pain in my arm is gone."

"He's backed off," Steve said, "but he hasn't left. Unfortunately, it doesn't feel as though anyone has left." The cook was still very much in command of her kitchen and she wasn't intending on relinquishing it any time soon.

When we explained that to Kirsten, she shrugged. "Now that I know it isn't anything evil, I can live with her." She looked around the room. "Just don't keep criticizing how I cook," she said aloud. "My family likes it and that's all that counts." Having said her peace, she turned to us.

"I told my upstairs neighbors you guys were coming and they were hoping you could go up to see them. They've been having issues and want to see what you get."

Upstairs

We trudged upstairs to the third floor and knocked on the door. It was opened by a thin, pretty blonde.

"Mandy, this is the group I was telling you about," Kirsten explained. We introduced ourselves and were led into a smaller, stylishly decorated apartment. In the living room, we were introduced to Mandy's husband, Peter. He was tall with dark hair and a dark goatee. Walking about the apartment were two Siamese cats who were eyeing us up and down.

"So what's been happening?" Steve asked.

Peter led us to a small room in the front of the house where he and Mandy kept their computers. "I do a lot of work on my computer and there are times that they go haywire. There's no rhyme or reason to it. I've troubleshooted to make sure there's nothing mechanically wrong and I always come up empty."

"There's also a feeling I get when I'm in here alone," Mandy added. "It's as if there's an angry man standing over me. I can't explain it, but it gets so overwhelming that I have to leave. Then there's the fact that ever since we moved in two months ago, Peter's developed a chronic cough. We've had the place checked for mold and anything else that might be causing his coughing. But we can't figure out why he's coughing as much as he is."

"I take it you don't smoke," Becky asked.

Peter shook his head. "The weird thing is that when I'm not home or if we go away for a week-end, I'm fine. But when we get back here, I start coughing again."

Lisa had remained quiet throughout the entire conversation. She looked thoughtful as she looked around the room. Finally, she made her way through the small group and stood next to Steve. "This is strange," she said, "but I keep seeing white sheets hung up on a clothes line. I don't know if it means anything."

"I wonder if it has anything to do with this man I'm picking up on," Steve replied. "He's dressed in black and he's very thin. Almost skeletal." He absently rubbed his stomach. "And very strong willed. He's just about crushing my third chakra. See if you guys pick up on him."

We closed our eyes to concentrate. "He looks like a preacher to me," Becky said. Steve shuddered as a chill ran through him.

Suddenly, the energy in the room changed as several spirits came forward. "There's a crowd of people here. They look like farmers. They keep pointing to the sheets. Why?" Steve whispered, more to himself than to us. "What are they trying to tell us?"

"The preacher keeps yelling," Becky said, "I can't understand what he's saying, but he's holding what looks like a Bible and he's reading from it."

"Ah, a fire and brimstone type of preacher. My favorite kind," Steve half joked.

"He really seems to control these people," Joy added as we felt the preacher's energy moving through the room.

A surge of anger and hopelessness flashed through me. "He's keeping them here," I caught my breath as the realization hit me. "His energy is so strong he's not allowing them to move on."

"He controlled them in life, he's controlling them in death," Steve muttered. I turned to see his brow wrinkled in deep concentration.

"You know, I keep seeing dirty sheets," Joy spoke up. "I know Lisa said she saw white sheets, but the ones I'm seeing are dirty."

Suddenly, Steve's blue eyes popped open. "I get it now. The sheets both of you saw are a metaphor. Airing dirty laundry. That's what this man did. He aired his parishioners' dirty laundry!"

We felt our chests constrict in pain as the preacher railed against us.

"But why?" Mandy asked. "Why would he do such a thing? And what is he doing here in our apartment."

"I'm not sure yet."

We tried to reach out to the spirits of the parishioners, but the preacher continually interfered, blocking any attempts to communicate with them. He came up behind each of us, trying his best to physically possess us. We rebuffed him.

Suddenly, a few members of the team began to cough. We compared notes and found that we were experiencing similar burning sensations in our lungs. The coughing quickly grew more ragged.

"I think this guy died of tuberculosis or something similar," Becky gasped as she rubbed her upper chest to ease the pain. "My lungs are on fire."

"That would explain why Peter coughs whenever he comes home," Lisa said.

We gathered into our familiar prayer circle, including Mandy, Peter and Kirsten. Combining our wills and assisted by our spirit guides, we were able to release the hold the preacher had on his parishioners. One by one they moved into the Light, leaving only the preacher behind.

He refused to budge.

He was intent on keeping the details of why he'd betrayed his congregation's trust secret and was adamant in staying to make sure nothing was revealed. We made a few more efforts to convince him to let it go and move on, but to no avail. We left that evening, happy with the discoveries we'd made, but disappointed that we weren't able to convince several of the spirits to leave. All we could hope was that they'd at least leave the living alone.

Follow-Up

Two days later, Steve unexpectedly felt an overwhelming need to visit the local church located two blocks from Jonah and Kirsten's home. It was within walking distance of Lisa's house, so on a crisp late summer evening, they walked down to the white steepled church. Upon entering, Steve was drawn to a plaque sitting in a quiet corner away from the altar. To his surprise, he saw that it was dedicated to the soldiers from the town who'd fought in World War II. There was a list of names, and there, in the middle of the list, was Sergeant Thomas Richardson.

Steve and Lisa quietly read the names and silently thanked each and every one for the sacrifices they'd made. When they were done, they felt Richardson's spirit lift and cross over to the Light, happy in the knowledge that all he and his friends had given up, including the physical loss of his arm, had been acknowledged and remembered.

Meanwhile, spurred by curiosity regarding the preacher and what he'd done to his congregation, Becky threw herself into researching all she could on the history of the town. Several hours later, she stumbled upon a story that confirmed our findings.

In the mid-1800s, the town fathers decided to bring prosperity to their town by building businesses and housing for the employees of these businesses. The world was evolving from farming into the industrial age and they were determined to be a part of it. The only thing standing in their way was the farms. With large tracts of land that could accommodate several factories, the farmers needed to be convinced to sell their property. Many, whose land had been in their families for several generations, resisted.

According to the newspaper article that Becky found, diaries were recently unearthed which detailed the unscrupulousness of the town preacher. In exchange for convincing farmers to sell, he received a payout from the town fathers. When he too met with fierce resistance, he began to "air their dirty linen," revealing secrets he had been privy to as the town's spiritual advisor. There was a huge scandal, which was quickly quashed by the town government. A footnote added that soon after the scandal subsided, the preacher died of tuberculosis.

Of course, the town fathers won in the end. The land was bought up, and where once corn and vegetables grew in abundance, there now stood stores and suburban housing. The preacher, once so prevalent in his day, faded into history. But apparently, not from Mandy and Peter's apartment. Despite his refusal to leave, now that his secret had been discovered, he was not as disruptive as he'd once been. After our visit, Peter found he was no longer afflicted with the cough. A few months later, they bought a house and moved out. A year later, Kirsten and Jonah moved out as well.

Hopefully, the cook isn't instructing the new tenants how to cook.

Discernment

For anyone who has had experience with the paranormal, either as someone who has been haunted or as someone who communicates with the other side, discernment is the most important lesson you can ever learn. For example, just because you hear a voice that tells you they're a Guide, it doesn't necessarily mean they are. We've met many people who believe they're being guided by a higher being only to find out it's "just a dead guy," as we say. Or we will have hauntings where people believe it's a child, or a relative, only to discover, "it's just a dead guy." Just as there are tricksters in life, there are tricksters in death. Despite our years of training and experience dealing with the Other Side, we always question what we get. We go within to see how what we receive feels. Your head can lie to you – you can convince yourself of anything. But your body and heart don't lie. Listen to your body. Listen to your heart. If it doesn't feel right, don't go with it, no matter who is giving you the information. In our own personal healing practices, we always tell our clients, if it doesn't feel right to you, don't go with it.

Beware of psychics and readers who draw you in to make money. If they insist on seeing you on a daily basis, they're probably trying to make money off of you. Ideally, you should see a psychic every six months or so. If a reading is fear based, they're also probably trying to make money off you. A reading should be a healing experience. As upsetting as these unscrupulous people can be, they serve as a discernment lesson for you. If it doesn't feel right, don't go with it, no matter who you hear it from.

For those of you who use pendulums, keep in mind that you really don't know who is answering you from the Other Side. On the occasions that we do use pendulums, we always preface what we ask with the words "In the Name of the Light." However, even this doesn't guarantee you will be communicating with true Guidance. Just listen to your instincts. If it doesn't feel right, don't go with it. And never allow yourself to fall under the influence of a living (or dead) person who controls your life. True guidance cannot interfere with your free will. A true psychic will know this as well.

10

On Old Cape Cod

*E*ACH INVESTIGATION IS A LEARNING EXPERIENCE, not only in refining and enhancing our psychic and investigative skills, but in uncovering the many reasons spirits remain stuck. This particular investigation, which took place on Cape Cod, Massachusetts, was instrumental in teaching us how planes of existence co-exist and interact with each other, even if that interaction is only one-sided.

Many of our cases come to us through word of mouth. This case was no different. Dale Fletcher, a young, successful contractor, heard about us through a friend. Calling Steve, he invited the group to spend the night in a summer cottage he'd bought in Barnstable a few years before. With a family which included three children, his wife, Terri, and a golden retriever, he'd found the charming two-story cottage just steps from the ocean – the ideal place for his brood to spend the hot New England summers. Fully furnished and at a reasonable price, he quickly scooped it up. However, soon after moving in, he discovered that his family members weren't the only ones inhabiting the house.

Every night around midnight, Terri awakened to the sound of footsteps. They'd start in the master bedroom located on the second floor, resound down the corridor and enter a small bedroom near the staircase. She'd spend the night listening to the footsteps occurring like clockwork every two hours.

Dale joined his family on weekends, spending Monday through Friday at his job near Boston. Usually exhausted from a long week at work, he slept through the footsteps. However, when it was time for him to take his vacation, he too heard the unnerving sounds night after night. Unlike his wife, who grew more frightened, Dale tried to find a logical explanation for the sounds. The cottage itself had been built in the 1940s. Perhaps it was the lonely whistling of the night wind that blew off the ocean that caused the strange noises. Or the usual sounds of an older, cedar-shingled house settling.

They managed to make it through the first summer, convincing themselves there was nothing paranormal going on. They closed up the house for the winter and life returned to normal.

The second summer brought more unwelcome surprises to the family.

Terri began to catch glimpses of a tall, thin man out of the corner of her eye. He would always be upstairs, near the stairway.

The bedroom where the footsteps appeared to enter was a guest bedroom for the children of relatives who flocked down to spend weekends near the ocean. There were four twin beds in the room, two facing the doorway and two placed side by side against the inner wall. With anywhere from five to seven children playing together, they always chose the guest bedroom to play and rough house in. By the second summer, however, Dale noticed the children were no longer playing in that particular bedroom. In fact, they tried to avoid it altogether, choosing to sleep on the floor in his children's bedroom which was located across the hall. When he'd ask what was wrong, they would just shrug. But they continued to avoid the room.

One evening, his eldest son began to feel unwell. Rather than go to his room, he decided to flop down in the guest bedroom, choosing the bed closest to the door. The family was gathered downstairs, chitchatting and relaxing after a day at the beach. Suddenly, they heard a piercing scream. Before they could move, their son tore down the stairway, his face white with horror and fear. It took them a while to calm him down. When he was finally able to speak, he told them that just as he was drifting off to sleep, he felt something cold come up beside him. He couldn't move, couldn't speak. He dared not open his eyes. Then he felt the coldness move down the side to the bed until it stood near his feet. In an instant, the coverlet he'd covered himself with was forcefully yanked off him, sending him into a panicked retreat.

That was the last straw for Terri. Unable to deny any longer that their house was haunted, she refused to return to the summer cottage. To recoup his investment, he began to rent the house to summer tourists.

Yet he was very drawn to the house. Strangely, from the moment his family moved in, he couldn't bring himself to make changes to the second floor. He did put in a new bathroom on the first floor, but that was it, despite being a contractor. He kept the furnishings just as they were when the previous owners had lived there. He discovered the only piece of furniture they'd taken when they'd moved was a baby's high chair and a plaque that had hung on the backyard fence. Although his own children were well out of infancy, he was compelled to buy a baby's high chair and place it in the same spot the other one had been located. He couldn't explain any of this when he spoke to Steve.

The Investigation

We arrived at Dale's cottage just as the sun was going down over Nantucket Sound. That night, the team consisted of Steve, Lisa, Amy and me. The house itself was charming and similar to many Cape Cod homes with their cedar shingles turned gray by the elements and there were nautical decorations in the front yard. Dale was waiting for us — he was a tall, blonde man, with a friendly expression on his tanned face. Rather than being frightened by what was going on in his cottage, he was intrigued and curious.

"I'd like my family to be able to enjoy this house. After all, I bought it for them. But Terri won't come down anymore. I'd heard from a friend of mine what a great job you guys did clearing and blessing his house. I'm hoping you can do the same thing here."

"We'll do our best," Steve replied as we brought in our overnight bags and put them in the living room.

The downstairs was large, constructed in an open, airy way without walls separating the dining and living rooms. We entered into the living room which had a stone fireplace and two sofas facing each other. In the center, between the sofas, was a square, glass-topped coffee table. To the right was the stairs leading up to the second floor. To the left you stepped right into the dining room. It had a large square, oak table and chairs and in the corner was the baby high chair Dale had mentioned buying to Steve during their phone conversation. Through the dining room was the kitchen. Off the kitchen was the new bathroom Dale had installed. It was huge, with a new upright shower that featured the newest in jets and water propulsion.

Off the dining room was a glass-enclosed porch with white bamboo furniture and cushy cushions. It overlooked a surprisingly wide expanse of yard. Many houses on the Cape have small, compact yards, but Dale's yard could easily fit two more houses.

Overall, the energy throughout the downstairs was warm and comfortable. There were no indications of spirit activity. We walked throughout the downstairs, snapping off pictures and doing temperature readings, but it remained clear. Coming back into the living room, we started up the stairs. Halfway up, the energy changed. It became heavier. Uncomfortable. We stood on the landing and looked down the corridor. The paneling along the wall was dark, adding to the bleak atmosphere. The rooms still retained the air of the 1940s, as did the fixtures and tile work in the bathroom.

"I've been wanting to redo the entire second floor," Dale said as he came up behind us. "I'd like to tear down this paneling and expand some of the bedrooms."

"Why haven't you?" Steve asked.

He shrugged. "I don't know. I start to plan it, but then I stop. It's as if I can't."

Since the guest bedroom had four beds and seemed to be the center of the haunting, we decided to each take a bed and spend the night there. We bid good-night to Dale and began to make preparations for the evening ahead. I took a series of photographs and was surprised to see what appeared to be a tube of energy coming out of the floor in the corridor and go into one of the bedrooms.

The tube appeared in several pictures, then disappeared. I also noticed that in the first picture I took, where the tube first appeared, the bottom frame was dark. As if there was a mass of dark energy there. Then, in the next picture which I immediately shot afterwards, the darkness was gone, though the tube remained.

We decided to set up the camcorder on a chair in the corridor, right over the spot where the tube of energy seemed to be emerging from. We also set up an EMF meter on the bureau in the bedroom where we'd all be sleeping.

By this time it was late, and we were tired. I set the camcorder to record and turned the EMF meter on.

"I want to sleep in the bed where the boy had the covers yanked off," Amy replied as we began to choose the beds we'd sleep in.

Note the tube of energy behind Lisa's head.

The tube of energy continues in the hallway accompanied by a dark shadow at the base of the photo.

In this shot taken seconds after, the tube of energy remains, but the dark shadow is gone.

"You're a brave one," I remarked.

"Better you than me," Steve joked as he stretched his six-foot-two-inch frame in the small twin bed. "I need my beauty sleep."

"Then you'll be asleep for *hours!*" Lisa joked. We laughed and set about making ourselves comfortable.

"It's interesting how the energy up here is so different from the energy downstairs," Lisa continued as she lay back against the bed frame. "It's as though the energy downstairs is in the twenty-first century and the upstairs is still trapped in the 1940s."

"Which is even more interesting when you consider that much of the furniture and decorations downstairs are a lot older than they are on the second floor, but, like Lisa said, up here feels like I've stepped back in time," I pointed out.

Amy began to hum the theme song to the *Twilight Zone*. "Exactly!" I laughed. "It's as though we've stepped into an episode of the *Twilight Zone*."

We turned off the lights and lay down on the beds. We waited quietly, hoping to hear the footsteps. For about a half hour all we heard was the wind blowing outside and the house creaking. Against our wills, we started drifting off to sleep.

The quiet was suddenly shattered when we heard the unmistakable sound of the chair out in the corridor scraping along the floor. Amy and I leapt out of our beds and ran into the corridor.

To our stunned amazement, the chair was moved a few inches from where I'd set it. As if someone had moved it to get through. I immediately checked the camcorder.

"Damn it," I said as I reviewed the tape.

"What's up?" Amy asked.

I showed her. For thirty minutes, the camcorder silently recorded the corridor, capturing the sounds of the wind and our soft whispers in the bedroom. Then the camera is jostled, probably when the chair was moved.

After that, the camcorder is turned off.

I was shocked. The battery was still working. Someone or something had deliberately moved the small lever from the record position up to the off position.

Amy and I looked at each other.

"Wow," she whispered.

I moved the chair back in position, pressed the record button on the camcorder and went back into the bedroom. We told Steve and Lisa what we'd discovered. We were in the middle of discussing it when we all felt an energy come into the room. Immediately, the EMF meter lit up and beeped furiously. It lasted for a few seconds, then all went quiet again.

"So much for our slumber party," Lisa remarked as we tried to settle down again. Although we didn't hear the footsteps, the EMF meter went off in precisely forty-five minute intervals for the rest of the night.

By the time four a.m. rolled around, we'd managed to snatch a few moments of sleep. We all sat on Steve's bed to discuss what had transpired so far.

"Just before the EMF meter went off, I felt the presence of a woman come up beside me," Amy reported. "I had a sense of her touching my forehead, then she'd move away again. The weird thing is that she didn't feel like she was there. I've felt spirits touch me physically. Her touch was more like a memory than anything else."

"I kept feeling that woman as well," Steve said. "She'd stand in the doorway and look in on us. But you're right. She felt more like a residual energy than an actual spirit."

"Did anybody feel the man?" Lisa asked. "I felt him come to the door a couple of times."

"That must be the man Dale's wife has been seeing," I answered. "Did he feel as though he were physically here?"

Lisa thought for a moment, then nodded.

We looked at each other. There was something off about all this. We all agreed that the woman was residual energy. Yet someone had moved the chair, turned off the camcorder and caused the EMF meter to go off. So we also had a true haunting – the physical presence of a spirit. Both were happening at the same time.

"You know, I had the impression of a child being sick," Amy said. "I felt as though I were a little girl lying in my bed and my mother coming in to check up on me."

A light bulb went off in our heads. "That explains the footsteps being heard at almost the same time and at the same intervals every night," Steve said. "The mother was getting up from her bed in the master bedroom every hour, walking down the corridor and entering this bedroom to check on her sick child."

We all had a deep knowing that the little girl hadn't survived her illness. This was something we'd have to check up on after the investigation. In the meantime, we continued peeling back the layers of this unusual investigation.

"So is the man Lisa felt the husband of the woman?" I asked.

Steve closed his eyes for a moment. "I'm hearing the name George. Could be the child's father."

By this time, it was growing lighter outside and we felt the need to go out into the backyard. We put on our sweaters against the cool morning air and let ourselves out through the kitchen. We walked along the fence line until we came to the far corner of the yard. There, on the wooden post fence was the unmistakable imprint of where a

Steve stands before spot where we believe a memorial was hung for a dead child.

plaque had been. Below, in the grass, we could see the marks where a statue had once stood.

"Looks like it could have been some kind of a memorial," Lisa said.

"Makes sense," Steve concurred. He turned back to the house. "In fact, it's all starting to make sense."

"How so?" I asked.

"Let's go back up the bedroom. I want to say a prayer."

We trudged back upstairs, arranged ourselves in a circle on Steve's bed and held hands. Steve cleared his throat and began to speak.

> As we sit here Creator, we have a knowing of a soul, a man who lived his life well. He loved, he cherished, he nurtured his family and he strived to provide for them. And in this man's knowing in death, he still strives to bring that comfort to this space, guarding it, keeping it safe, making sure that changes do not happen so that those in his family will feel comfortable. But as we sit here with this man and his memories, we say to him that comfort does not reside in this house. The comfort resides in your heart. It is not by the wood, or the stone or the paint that the family felt safe in this place, but with every beat of your heart, every wink of your eye, every strong nurturing touch that you gifted

to each of them. For your presence was a rock to them in times of need and when their hearts were troubled or when their souls needed reassurance that all was fine. We ask in this moment that you release yourself from this house. We know that it's difficult. Allow this house which you cared for so deeply to be transferred to a new family. And if you so wish, you may gaze down upon them from a higher place, and see the love they hold for each other, and be reminded of your life. If there's a part of you who felt you didn't father your daughters well enough – know that they have their own journeys to follow. Know that you planted the seeds. Know that their choices must come from the same place from which you made your choices. Allow your fears to fade. Allow any guilt to fade. Allow any disappointment to fade. We ask that you leave with us this day. We are here to help. We are here to honor you. We are sent to gather those who have lived well and bring them home. Know that you are deserving of this. Leave this place with us. Join hands with your wife. Join hands with all your relations and begin the journey Home. Amen.

Follow-Up

After our visit, Dale discovered through a neighbor that a man named George had indeed built and lived in that house for many years. A devoted family man who adored his wife and four daughters, he'd lost his youngest, when she was two, to a fever. Upon the death of George and his wife, his remaining daughters immediately sold the house.

George's need to keep everything just as it had been when he was alive caused him to remain stuck when his physical body ceased to exist. His anger and disappointment that his daughters had sold the place that he'd loved so much also caused him to remain. What Steve did in his prayer was what we call Ghost Psychology. We brought all the energy that was in the house – his energy and the energy he was using to keep the image of his wife and dying daughter in place – to a center point where we were able to stop it. We then had George face reality. His wife and daughter were gone. The house was gone, but it had gone to a family who would love and nurture it and create their own loving memories in it just as George and his family had done.

We were able to convince him to let it all go. Yet, there were still emotions he needed to work through before he could be free to continue his journey Home. Steve elected to work with George and a week later, George did go Home. Two months after our visit, Dale's family stayed at the house and reported all was well. No footsteps, nothing to disrupt their sleep or their visit. Dale is once again busy making plans to redo the house. He feels nothing holding him back. He is ready to make the house theirs.

Working with a Spirit

In several of these stories, you will have noticed that we take turns "working with a spirit." What this means is that at the time of the investigation, a spirit may not be ready at that point to go Home. Unless a spirit is deliberately interfering with the living, we don't force them to go Home. Just as they had free will in life, we respect their free will in death. However, we find that after we do our circles, the spirit will attach itself to us. They know they have an opportunity to leave the in-between place, which is neither of this World or the next. One of us will volunteer to continue to work with the spirit – feeling their emotions, counseling them, reassuring them that it's okay to continue their journey Home. What we do is show them that they have a choice. They can continue to stay in the darkness of the in-between place, or move to a place of love and peace. After we have worked through their emotions and traumas, many choose love and peace. Wouldn't you?

11

The Old Manse

THE OLD MANSE IN CONCORD, MASSACHUSETTS has been a historical landmark for many years. It was built in 1770 for the minister of Concord, Reverend William Emerson, and his wife, Phebe. They lived in the home for six years and were present when the battle for independence took place in April 1775 in a field behind their home near the North Bridge.

If the name Emerson sounds familiar, it's because one of William and Phebe's children became the father of the American poet Ralph Waldo Emerson.

Unfortunately, William Emerson died of camp fever in 1776, and two years later, his widow married the Reverend Ezra Ripley. It was their son Samuel, who in 1842, rented the Old Manse to the writer Nathaniel Hawthorne and his wife, Sophia. They lived there for three years, remembering that time as the happiest years of their lives.

Our favorite investigations are those that take place in old historical houses. Not only do we enjoy the written history of the place, but we are also intrigued by the unwritten history as well. Using our psychic abilities, we've had occasion to uncover facts that are not well known and which have later been confirmed by family diaries or family lore.

The Old Manse was no different.

A Dandy

Steve and I were invited to visit the Old Manse to conduct a private ghost investigation by Cathryn McIntyre. Cathryn is a published writer and independent researcher who not only has studied the life and work of writer Henry David Thoreau, but also has an extensive knowledge of Concord's vast literary history. As a natural psychic herself and a friend of Steve's, she wondered what we would pick up in this almost 250-year-old house.

It was around 6 p.m., in May of 2010, that Steve, Amy, our newest member, Michelle Johnson, and I arrived at the Old Manse.

Because of her extensive work as a tour-guide in several historical mansions, we thought Michelle would enjoy this private tour. As it happened, she didn't know much about the Old Manse. In fact, none of us did. Having once served as a tour guide at the North Bridge next door to the Manse, I could recite the history of April 19, 1775 in my sleep. But I was lost when it came to knowing the history of the Old Manse.

Driving through the quiet, tree-shaded streets of Concord, Steve began to feel a sense of anger and resentment towards "that dandy." He then saw the image of a man filter through his third eye. He described a young man with mutton-style sideburns, wearing a high collar and cravat, and sporting a head of thick, wavy hair. I inwardly smiled. That fit the description of a typical Victorian-era gentleman and could apply to anyone. As usual, we filed it away in hopes that as the evening progressed, we would discover what these images and emotions meant.

A light rain was falling and the air was cool as we parked our car in the visitors' parking area. We slowly made our way over the carefully cared-for grounds and around the house in an attempt to get a feel for whatever might be around.

We felt nothing except a deep sense of peace. We entered the side door right into the gift shop. There we met Cathryn and the Director

A shot of the front of the historical Old Manse in Concord, MA.

of the Old Manse who had graciously allowed us complete access to the house for the evening.

A tall woman with dark blonde hair and intelligent eyes, Cathryn was well acquainted with the house. She would be our tour guide for the evening, taking notes of our findings, confirming what she could and conducting further research if the need arose. The gift shop itself was small and crammed with books on all aspects of the literary and social history of Concord. They were also displaying its newest line of T-shirts that featured a picture of Nathaniel Hawthorne with the statement "Hawthorne was a Hottie".

I had to admit they were right. Hawthorne was incredibly handsome. When Steve saw the T-shirt, he pointed to it.

"That's the vision I had in the car. That's who I saw."

The description Steve had given us in the car and the picture on the T-shirt were a perfect match. Hawthorne did indeed look a bit like a dandy.

"There is it again," Steve murmured. "I can feel the energy of someone who really resents him."

"Any idea who?" Michelle asked.

The question remained unanswered.

"Hawthorne was a Hottie."

Cathryn slowly led us through the kitchen and into the dining room. There on the wall was a copy of an 1840's portrait of Hawthorne.

"I can't even look at the picture without feeling hostile," Steve said. This continued to be the theme of the tour as we walked through the rooms. In the study, we came across an etching made on the old glass of one of the windows that overlooked the field abutting the North Bridge.

"Hawthorne's wife, Sophia, used her diamond ring to write love messages to her husband," Cathryn explained.

We went up to one of the windows and read, "Man's accidents are God's purposes."

"We think we know what that may refer to, but I'll wait to see what else you pick up," Cathryn said with a mysterious twinkle in her eye.

Steve stood in the middle of the room and closed his eyes to concentrate. "It feels as though the man who resents Hawthorne

We captured this strange anomaly on the couch in what was once the parlor in the Old Manse.

doesn't like the way he's being remembered. In fact, there are a few spirits here who are telling me that Hawthorne isn't quite the romantic figure everyone believes him to be."

Cathryn had trouble with this revelation. Like thousands, she had read the countless stories that portrayed Hawthorne as a handsome romantic figure who was deeply in love with his wife and devoted to his writing. Time and time again, it has been stated in the written record that the three years he spent at the Old Manse with Sophia were the happiest of their lives.

So why did the spirits of the Old Manse resent him so much?

We decided to move on to the third-floor attic space. There were several, unfinished rooms at the top of the house and we had to be careful where we stepped. In a small room to the right of the stairway that may have once served as a bedroom, Steve began to receive more information.

"The resentment seems to be coming from two sources. One source has to do from the days he rented this place. It's coming from a male spirit who's very adamant about the fact that Hawthorne was a lousy tenant. The other seems to be coming from a female. She's telling me about a party that took place at the house with the large porch around it. It's gray and rambling.

I get the sense Hawthorne may have owned it, or had something to do with it. Do you know if Hawthorne was ever associated with such a house?"

Cathryn thought for a moment. "There was only one house that Hawthorne ever owned. It's the Wayside Inn in Sudbury. It does have a large wrap around porch now, though it wasn't there at the time Hawthorne owned it."

"This woman is telling me about the porch so we recognize which house it is."

"What happened there?" Michelle asked.

"Something happened at the Wayside that upset this woman greatly. It either happened to her or to someone she knew. But the end result is that a woman ended up getting pregnant there. And she wasn't married."

"That would have been scandalous in those days," I remarked. "It would have ruined the woman's life."

"That sounds very much like the plotline from *The Scarlet Letter*, one of Nathaniel Hawthorne's more successful novels," Cathryn pointed out. "It's the story of a puritan woman who has an affair with the minister and ends up getting pregnant. She's forced to wear the letter 'A' sewn to her bodice to show the world of her adultery. Hawthorne always maintained that he'd come across documentation in the Old Customs House in Salem indicating that such an event had actually taken place. He used that as the foundation for his story."

Steve shook his head. "I'm being told by this woman that the story came to him in another way."

After that, the spirit of the woman refused to say more.

We continued our walk through the attic. In one of the front rooms that overlooked the main drive, Steve saw the image of a woman standing at the window, looking out over the drive. It felt as though this was her favorite room and she had stood at that window many, many times. In the same room, I began to get bits and pieces of a name. I couldn't quite get it all. It sounded like Rush or Rusha. I continued to try and connect and finally I got the name "Jerusha". It was an unusual name and I turned to Cathryn.

"Ever heard of a Jerusha? She feels very puritan to me."

"Well, the house was built in 1770, well after the puritan era."

"She could be attached to the land. But she's making it very clear that her name is Jerusha."

Cathryn made note of the name and told us she'd look into it. At this point, Michelle began to pick up on the name Frances.

A few moments later, Amy, Michelle, and I felt the unmistakable symptoms of being pregnant. I felt as though I'd given birth several times, my insides stretched and uncomfortable. I've never had a child, but I wasn't surprised at feeling what I did when one considered the time period we were tuning into that had scant knowledge, if any, of birth control.

Michelle began to feel intense labor pains and had to sit down to ground out the discomfort.

"Oh dear," she said, her green eyes welling with tears. "I feel as though I've lost a baby." She glanced down at her belly. "The woman I'm feeling around me had a miscarriage. She's absolutely devastated."

Cathryn's eyes widened. "Do you remember that saying you saw etched downstairs on the windowpane? The one that said "Man's accidents are God's purposes?" We nodded. "It's believed that Hawthorne's wife, Sophia, wrote that after suffering a fall which resulted in a miscarriage in 1843."

With that as good confirmation, we shed the vestiges of childbirth and pregnancy pain and finished our tour of the attic. Nothing else jumped out at us and we decided to return downstairs to the nursery. It was a small room with a long table where we all sat. Cathryn immediately picked up on a female spirit who she identified as Theodora Thayer. She was familiar with this spirit, having encountered her before during one of her many visits to the Old Manse. Steve picked up on her as well. Turning, he saw her

Michelle picks up on the name "Frances" who was later revealed to be a woman who spent much time at the Old Manse.

portrait on the wall and confirmed that she was one of the spirits haunting the Old Manse.

"She's drawn to you because you share the same feminist attitudes she did," Steve explained to Cathryn. "It's an example of like energy attracting like energy."

Cathryn nodded. "That makes sense. When I first encountered her, I felt certain that she followed me home. I tried to talk to her and convince her to let go of whatever it was that was holding her back and to move on. I thought I'd convinced her, but later I discovered that she'd simply returned here."

Amy suddenly shuddered. "She's telling me that a member of her family attempted to "show her what she was missing." She's very upset about it. Do you have any idea what that could mean?"

A look of intense sorrow crossed over Cathryn's face. "Oh God, I hope not," she whispered. She took a moment to compose herself, then looked up at us. "When I first encountered her spirit, I didn't know much about Theodora, so I started doing some research. The Ripleys married into the Thayer family in the mid 1800s. Theodora was born in 1868. She became a successful artist of miniature paintings, living an independent life in New York City. It was believed she was a lesbian." She shook her head. "As distressing as it was, what you just heard may explain why she suddenly committed suicide in August of 1905. She was only in her mid-30s."

"She's saying that she does not wish to cross because she doesn't want to encounter family members or give up the freedom she has now. This is her freedom. She can come and go as she pleases and answers to no one," Steve said.

"I understand that completely," Cathryn admitted. "I've never wanted to commit to anyone. My writing is what is important to me. Probably like Theodora, marriage to me means surrendering my own needs and desires." She looked around her. "So many women who lived in this house had no control over their lives. They married and had child after child. If they'd wanted to experience a life outside of here, it could only be done through their husbands and even that was limited. Theodora had the courage to strike out on her own and live the life she wanted to live."

"She's going to come home with you again," Steve revealed to Cathryn. "If you want, you can help her work through whatever it is that's holding her back. Hopefully that will allow her to finally cross."

"How do I do that?"

"You allow her to meld her emotions with yours. Experience those emotions and attitudes that you both share. Not only will you help her to release what's holding her back, it may also help you release what's holding you back as well."

Cathryn looked startled for a moment, then quietly nodded.

It was getting late, but there was one other room we wished to revisit. We'd all felt the pull to return to the master bedroom, and, in particular, to a portrait there of an auburn haired woman with sad eyes and a somber expression on her pretty face. Cathryn pointed out that this was Una Hawthorne, daughter of Nathaniel and Sophia, who had been born in that room in March of 1844.

We entered the beautifully decorated bedroom and looked at the sketch of Una. Before Cathryn could tell us the story of this Hawthorne descendent, we all began to feel what can best be described as erratic behavior. There were emotional highs, followed by deep, depressing lows. We felt sadness, fear, and regret that her short life had been dominated by illness and heartache. There was also desperation on Una's part to find a child, though whether this was a child she had or thought she'd had, we couldn't tell. However, we were overwhelmed by her manic despondency. I kept hearing her telling me over and over again, "Please don't tell... Please don't tell." She seemed torn between wanting to tell us and hoping that no one would ever know. Before we could try to figure out how to help this very troubled spirit, another spirit – this one male – entered the room.

There was a series of photographs laid out on the bed and Steve pointed to one as being the male spirit that had just made his appearance. Cathryn identified the photo as that of Julian, Una's younger brother. As Steve tuned into him, he related that Julian was there to protect Una, though whether it was to protect her from us, or protect her from revealing whatever this secret was that she was holding onto, we couldn't tell.

Cathryn confirmed the erratic emotions we were feeling. Una had always been considered an artistic, yet eccentric, child. As she grew older, her mental state grew more precarious. This was helped along by the death of her parents, and several broken romances, including the death of her fiancé who died on a voyage to Honolulu, ironically to improve his health. After his untimely death, she seemed to have withered away and she died at the young age of 33.

By this time, the hour was very late and we decided we'd done all we could. We thanked the Director for allowing us such a wonderful experience exploring this interesting house that had seen so much history. Cathryn promised she would look into the historical record to test the accuracy of what we'd gotten. We then bid a fond farewell to the Old Manse and took off into the night.

Follow-Up

A few days later, Cathryn contacted Steve and shared the following information she'd been able to dig up.

It appears that Hawthorne was indeed a poor tenant. They carved etchings onto the window glass and put a hole in the kitchen wall to accommodate a modern stove, actions done without consulting the owners. They were also months behind on their rent and they were finally asked to leave by the Ripley family. Although it was the Ripley family that owned the home since the demise of William Emerson and gave the house to the Trustees of Reservations in 1939, the house still continues to be known as the Hawthornes' home. Could this be why the male spirit Steve first felt upon our arrival at the Manse feels hostility towards Nathanial Hawthorne? Is he upset because it's known as the Hawthornes' home and not as the Ripley House?

The woman standing in the window on the third floor may have been the spirit of Sarah Ripley. According to a memoir that Cathryn read the day after our investigation, it was revealed that Sarah used that room as a nursery and spent countless hours in there, looking out that very window.

Cathryn also discovered the name Jerusha three times in the Emerson/Ripley family tree. The first was born in 1699 and died in 1783. The second was born in 1734 and died in 1812. And the third was Sarah Ripley's aunt, born 1770 and died 1833. Because of the puritan energy I'd picked up with the name, we wondered if our Jerusha may have been the one born in 1699.

During her research, Cathryn found a photograph of the Ripley family taken in the front yard of the Manse in 1882. Pictured with the family was a woman named Frances Ames Randall. Could this be the Frances that Michelle picked up on in the attic? After studying the photograph, Cathryn is convinced that many of those pictured are still haunting the Manse.

The last and most interesting piece of information that Cathryn uncovered had to do with Theodora. Drawn as she is to Theodora, she has done and continues to do much research into her life, especially on the events that led up to her untimely death. What she discovered was a remark made and referenced in a biography of a fellow artist of Theodora's named Eulabee Dix. According to this remark, the Thayer family was very successful in covering up the circumstances of Theodora's death. What was it that the family fought so hard to hide? Interestingly enough, her brother took his own life ten years after Theodora's death. His suicide was attributed to depression. But was there a darker reason? Was he the one who felt he had to "show her what she was missing"? And is this the reason the family fought so hard to cover up the circumstances surrounding Theodora's suicide?

Until something turns up in the written record to confirm our findings, it will remain a mystery.

To those who believe, there is no need of proof. To those who don't believe, there is never enough.

Look at Other Alternatives

For those of you who might be interested in investigating haunted places, or who have had experiences with the Other Side, keep in mind two things. A person doesn't need to have died in a location to haunt that location. In life they may have been attached to a place and in death they return to it. As you've seen in these stories, you also may be a haunted person yourself and you will attract spirits to yourself through no effort of your own. You may be sitting in your living room one evening, with no particular thought or emotion and suddenly you feel angry or agitated for no reason at all. There's a good possibility that a spirit has entered your energy field. Use the grounding and centering techniques I've outlined in the book to assist that spirit. They may not cross, but you can help lighten them up.

If you are exploring historical areas, remember that not everything is written in the historical record. There are many "skeletons in the closet." Just because you may feel something that wasn't written about doesn't mean it didn't happen. As in the Old Manse, we can only go by what we felt. Of course, it's wonderful if we do find historical confirmation. But again, don't completely discount a discovery just because someone didn't feel it proper to write about a scandal or a potential scandal. There are always emotional facts that may not correspond with the written facts. If you are psychic or sensitive to energy, keep digging to get behind the known story. You'll never know what you might turn up.

12

Drama in Life and Death

"THE HOUSE ITSELF WAS BUILT IN 1690 and it's had quite a colorful history. In the '60s, it was owned by a record producer. The Grateful Dead used to come over whenever they were in the area and crash. When we were cleaning the basement, we found all sorts of drug paraphernalia!"

Leah laughed while we tried our best not to get caught in the vast array of spider webs strung along the low basement ceiling.

"I think I heard somewhere that the producer and his wife started having problems while they lived here. They ended up getting divorced."

We'd been called out to investigate the home of Leah and Alexander Stein and their eight-year-old son, Carl, transplanted New Yorkers who'd bought the old home a year before. Leah, who was a believer in the paranormal and a dedicated practitioner of feng shui heard about us through a mutual friend. She'd known the house was haunted from the beginning and thought she could get along with the spirits. However, she came to the conclusion that they were interfering in her life, specifically in her desire to have another child. Knowing it was time to try and cleanse the house of the disruptive energy, she phoned Steve.

Strong Wills

It was a drizzly and cool September evening when Steve, Amy, Becky, our newest investigator-in-training Joanne Martel, and I drove through the dark, forest-lined road to the Steins' house.

When we pulled up to the large rambling red house, we were met by both a large goose who stared us down in the driveway and the heavy, oppressive energy settling into our chests and stomachs.

We piled out of Becky's van and found ourselves with an unusual problem. There were several doors into the house and we weren't sure which one to use. We walked around, trying to find a doorbell. With each step, the heaviness in our bodies grew. We each unconsciously rubbed our upper chests and stomachs to try and relieve the discomfort. Not only was the heaviness due to the presence of a spirit, but it also indicated an extremely strong will, not only of the spirit, but of Leah as well.

Surrounding the house, the dense forest seemed to be creeping in on us. I looked around, but could see nothing but inky blackness.

"I always wonder how people survived without electricity," I mused as we continued to try and find the right door. "It's pitch black out there."

"I can't imagine living without my iPod," Becky joked. "Gotta listen to my music!"

"Heelllooooo!"

We turned to see a short, rotund woman, with graying hair pinned in the back with a barrette, materialize from behind the house. Although the evening was cool, she was dressed in shorts and a T-shirt.

"You said you'd be here at 7:30. It's now 7:33."

We smiled to ourselves. Strong-willed, indeed!

"We had to swing by and pick up Amy. Hello, I'm Steve."

We did the introductions and I was struck by how powerful a handshake she had.

"Come in through the kitchen," she commanded as she turned on her heel and retraced her steps to the back of the house.

Because of her dedication to the principles of feng shui, I was expecting an interior of furnishings placed in strategic locations to allow the "chi" or energy to flow throughout each room.

What we found was something entirely different.

The New England area had just gone through Tropical Storm Irene. It looked as though the storm had personally passed through every room in Leah's house. Although she told us the family had moved in a year before, the disarray made it appear as though they'd moved in the day before. Along with the heaviness we continued to feel, a walkthrough revealed that the energy was also scattered and unfocused. Part of this was Leah's personal energy. But part of it was something else – the unfocused and frenetic energy coming from another source that was actually intertwining with and overcoming Leah herself.

Carefully stepping over papers, toys, boxes, and a vacuum cleaner that lay in the middle of a doorway, I saw the figure of a tall, extremely thin man dressed in black. He was stern and uncompromising and he made it clear to me that he didn't like Leah being in "his" house. The other members also picked up on this man and we concluded he was the source of the heavy oppressive energy we were feeling. While Amy, Becky, and Joanne spread out to the other rooms, Steve and I remained in the kitchen with Leah. It was there that Steve made contact with the black-clad gentleman.

"He's telling me about the Millerite movement. And he's very angry about it. Hey Bety, do you know when the Millerite movement took place?"

"I think it was the 1840s," I replied.

We had encountered this particular movement in a previous investigation and were able to share its details with Leah.

The Millerite movement was based on the preachings of William Miller, a farmer from upstate New York, who was convinced that Christ would be returning to earth in 1843. His beliefs reached a national audience through the use of leaflets and his movement exploded. People, convinced that the end of times was coming, sold or gave away their property. It all cumulated in what has come down in history as "The Great Disappointment." The date of October 22, 1844 was chosen as the last day of Earth. When that didn't happen, other dates in April, July and October of 1845 were chosen. Those dates came and went, leaving many in the movement disillusioned. An interesting footnote to all this was the rarity in which those who had given away their property were able to get it back once they realized the end times wasn't arriving any time soon.

"His wife was involved with the Millerites," Steve continued. A chill of anger flew through us. "Whew. No wonder he hated them. His wife tried to give their property away."

"So he's the one with the angry energy," Leah concluded.

"Yes. His family owned this property for many generations and the last thing he was going to allow was his wife giving away the family legacy to a movement he had no belief or trust in."

"Why don't you show us around the house?" I asked. "We may pick up more as we go."

Leah led the way and as I followed, I found my shoulder suddenly aching. Then my body began to ache. Meeting up with Joanne in the hallway, she complained of a headache. "What's weird is that I can't lift my head," she whispered to me. "I feel as though I have to keep my eyes focused on the ground."

"Like you're being submissive?" I asked.

"Yeah, something like that. Look. See what I mean?"

She attempted to lift her head, but couldn't.

"Who do you think it is?"

"It feels like a female. She's dressed in white." Joanne started to rub her belly. "It feels really uncomfortable. Painful."

I wondered if she had picked up on the spirit of the woman who had been a follower of the Millerites. I kept silent, not wanting to taint her own psychic impressions.

We continued the tour throughout the downstairs, upstairs, and attic. When we reached the basement, she showed us the room where the Grateful Dead had once hung out. I got the distinct

The glamorous life of a ghosthunter.

feeling that somewhere in the stone foundation were hidden papers. I couldn't get any information on who had placed them there or why, or what these papers contained, but throughout the evening, I couldn't shake the feeling that something was hidden in one of the myriad of niches.

The man in black was never far behind as we finished the tour of the house. Steve then asked Leah to show us the outside. Amy and Joanne opted to remain inside and do some EVP work so Becky, Steve, Leah, and I ventured out into the light drizzle that was beginning to fall.

We walked towards a structure set apart from the house that Leah called the barn. Suddenly, Steve stopped. "1862. I keep seeing the year 1862. And the name Anna."

"I don't know where it is yet; I haven't found it," Leah replied. "But there's a stone somewhere around here that marks the spot where an Edward Ellis dropped dead."

A shiver ran down our spines. "I just got a chill when you said that name," Steve said. "That's the man dressed in black who's been following us. And the name 'Anna' I keep hearing is that of his wife."

"The one who fell in with the Millerites?" Becky asked.

"Yes."

I looked back to the old house. "Ever since we got here, we've been getting physical aches and pains." I turned back to Steve and Leah. "I think this Ellis guy beat his wife."

This time the shivers extended to Leah, followed by a deep sense of guilt.

"I'm curious about the frenetic, almost crazy energy that's in the house as well," I said. "I can't quite put my finger on it, but it's all over the place."

"I'm not surprised. The woman we bought the place from actually went insane in this house. She embezzled some money from her job which ended up wrecking her marriage and causing her to sink into mental illness." Leah paused. "I often wonder if that's why I have so much trouble staying focused. I know it's hard to believe, but I'm actually a very organized person. At least I was until we moved here."

"Is the woman who went insane still alive?" I asked.

"Yes, I believe so. She obviously couldn't take care of herself so her daughter took her in."

It was not surprising that the energy in the house felt so scattered, or why Leah was having a hard time focusing her attentions on what needed to be done around the house. Although the previous owner was still alive, the type of energy generated by her descent into madness was strong enough to stay within its walls. With someone as sensitive as Leah now living there and unwittingly allowing her own energies to be overtaken by those of the previous owner, it was anchoring that dramatic dysfunction.

"Let's get the rest of the team," Steve spoke up. "I'd like to say a prayer."

We gathered the group and stood outside the front door, which was actually located on the left side of the house. We held hands and Steve began the process of allowing Edward and Anna to forgive themselves. We then went inside to the spot that Leah considered the heart of the house. There, Steve said another prayer, allowing the house to now be filled with the energies of Leah and her family. He asked that all other energies be cleared and that Leah now take possession of her home. When we were done, Leah, with tears in her eyes, gave us each a strong hug.

"It's unbelievable how much better it feels in here," she murmured.

"I don't know why, but I have to go back into the living room," Joanne said. Without waiting for a response, she turned and hurried through the doorway. When I followed a few moments later, I found her kneeling in front of one of the original fireplaces. She was bent over and silently sobbing. I knew Anna had merged her energies with Joanne and Joanne was reliving a traumatic moment in Anna's life.

We gathered around Joanne and held space for her to live through Anna's pain and anguish, knowing this would help Anna relinquish the heavy energy that was keeping her here.

"It's so sad," Joanne wept. "I feel like he beat her here. In front of the fireplace." She covered her face with her hands. "She was pregnant. I can see the blood. Oh my God, she lost the baby."

I turned to Leah. "That may be why you can't get pregnant. That loss and the anger and guilt surrounding the event was still here, interfering with you and your energy."

After a few moments of heartfelt weeping, Joanne slowly regained her composure. Exhausted by her ordeal, she flopped down on the couch.

"Welcome to the group," Steve smiled.

"You mean that was some kind of initiation?"

"In a way. We've all been through it. In time, you'll learn not to get so immersed in a spirit's energy and just allow it to move through you."

Meanwhile Leah was going through a pile of papers in the corner of the room. She withdrew an 8" x 14" photograph and handed it to us.

"Although I haven't found the stone yet, here's a picture of it."

It was indeed a photograph of a stone slab. Carved in the style of writing popular in the nineteenth century, it read:

Here on this spot died Edward Ellis
Age **62**
Of a Mowing
August 14, **18**48

The numbers 62 and 18 were prominent and stuck out from the rest of the carving.

"Hey, there's the 1862 I saw!" Steve exclaimed.

"He died of mowing?" Becky asked.

"They had to do it by hand back then," I explained. "In the heat of the summer and his advanced age, he probably suffered a heart attack."

By this time Leah had pulled up a genealogy chart. "You were right about Anna. She was married to Edward and died a few years after he did." She leaned back against the sofa. "You know, when we decided to move up here, this was the first house we looked at. As soon as I saw it, I didn't want to look at anything else. I knew this was the place for me."

"We've seen that in other investigations," Steve explained. "You were drawn to this house because you were meant to help those who are still here. It's interesting how there's a thread running through this

Joanne, Amy and Becky just before Joanne becomes possessed by the spirit of an abused woman.

house – strong women who had issues with their marriages. Edward Ellis, the record producer, the woman who went insane. Looks like you were meant to be here to break that thread."

The hour was late and it was time to leave. We said our good-byes and piled back into Becky's van.

"In all the investigations we've done, that has got to be the most communicative ghost I've ever met," Steve related as we made our way down the darkened road.

"We certainly got some good confirmations on what you were getting," Amy agreed.

"I'll be curious to see if Leah finds these hidden papers I kept seeing all night," I said. I turned to Joanne. "Are you feeling better?" I asked.

She nodded. "As soon as I walked into the house, I felt her with me. That was so weird not being able to lift my head up. I still feel a bit heavy, though it's not as bad as it was."

"You were moving a lot of energy for her. Guess you'll be taking Anna home to continue the process of helping her to get Home."

She laughed. "So I'm now an official member of the team, huh?"

Follow-Up

The prayer to clear the dark and frenetic energy was successful. Leah has taken back her home and is in the process of applying her feng-shui knowledge to each room. She is also pursuing her heart-felt wish of becoming pregnant again. We wish her the very best.

What Keeps This Energy Going?

Drama in life equals drama in death. There are no truer words when it comes to paranormal investigations. Death does not stop the drama. Edward Ellis' life was certainly dramatic, starting with the Millerite movement, the near loss of his property, the beating of his wife, and the loss of their baby. The record producer's life was dramatic, as well as the woman who eventually went insane in the house. Which begs another question. What kept this energy going over the years? It was the drama of the living feeding into the drama of the dead. Energy cannot be destroyed, but it can be changed. The continual feeding of the energy of drama by the living created an ambiance where anyone who was even the least bit sensitive would be affected to the point where, like Leah, it was overpowering her own energy and she found herself getting caught up in the frenetic, unfocused, and heavy atmosphere around her. She and others before her fed into the initial dramatic energy, amplifying it and keeping it going like logs on a fire.

As in other investigations we've conducted over the years, we've noticed there are people like Leah who are drawn to a location, not because they like it, but because they're meant to change the energy in some way. Through our help, Leah was able to break the cycle of the dysfunctional energy and claim the space as hers. The trick for her, and others like her, will be to stay out of drama. Change your energy and the energy around you changes as well.

Afterword

I SINCERELY HOPE THAT YOU ENJOYED THE STORIES I've presented here. They are all true. We have only changed the names and locations of our clients to preserve their privacy.

It is The Spirit Light Network's mission to educate the public, not only about life after death, but about the dynamics of energy. I've endeavored to show, as clearly as possible, techniques that you can start incorporating into your everyday life to improve that life. It's not easy in the world today, but you have a choice. You can allow yourself to become immersed in all the fear and drama. You can leak your energy and become prey to both the living and the dead who feed on that energy, leaving you exhausted and apathetic. Or you can try to keep your vibration high. Remember, your energy affects others. It is the equivalent of throwing a pebble into a pond. It ripples out. The more you heal yourself, the more your vibration rises and the brighter your personal light becomes. It radiates out and can't help but affect other people.

Everything that occurs in our lives serves as a lesson. It's how you choose to react to these occurrences that determine whether something will continue to occur over and over again, be it bad relationships, bad jobs, bad self-esteem or whether you can finally nip it in the bud. Sometimes all it takes is a simple shift in your energy to start attracting what you want into your life.

Ghosts occur because these people chose to remain immersed in their fears and dramas. Their vibrations were low at time of death and they didn't achieve the energetic threshold they needed in order to cross over into the Light. In each of these stories, I've tried to show the varying reasons why people remain stuck, from the woman who wanted the head of her tombstone returned to the man on Cape Cod who needed to keep everything the same for the sake of the family he loved so much.

Of course not every ghost is stuck. There are many who know they can continue on their journey, but choose to remain, for a little while, to look after loved ones or to help them through the grieving process.

The bottom line is to try and lead the most fulfilling life you can. Heal all that you can heal. Trust that what happens in your life needs to happen to teach you an important lesson. Learn from those lessons. As hard as it is to believe when you're in the depths of despair or sadness, it really is all good. An opportunity has presented itself to shake off the chains of dysfunctional energy that no longer serve you. Feel your anger, your hurt, your pain. Then move on. Keep your vibration high as much as you can so when your time comes, you don't become a ghost yourself.

For more information on The Spirit Light Network, or if you have a location that you would like investigated, or if you'd just like to share your comments about this book or experiences you'd had with the Other Side, contact us at gotghost2006@yahoo.com or visit our website at www.spiritlightnetwork.net. We'd love to hear from you.

Appendix: Lessons

IN ORDER TO MAKE IT EASIER FOR YOU to quickly look up and use any of the Shamanic techniques I've described in each chapter, each lesson is repeated, in its entirety in the following Appendix. Enjoy!

Grounding

Grounding is a technique where you literally ground out any emotions, whether yours or someone else's that adversely affect you and keep you from feeling your best. This is an especially important technique to learn if you are sensitive to other people's emotions or if you feel overwhelmed by crowds or heavy emotions. Close your eyes and imagine a round red ball about a foot beneath the soles of your feet. Focus your attention on this red ball. The more you focus on this ball, the more you should begin to feel your emotions slowly moving from your head, down through your chest and stomach, slowly cascading down your abdomen and legs and out the bottom of your feet into this ball. You may feel your feet tingling and you will begin to feel lighter the more you do this. Grounding really is that simple. The more you do this, the more you will train your body to automatically ground.

A Simple Way to Balance Yourself

Start by placing your left hand over your heart and your right hand over your belly (your heart is considered the fourth chakra [chakras are energy points in our bodies that hold emotions] and your belly is your third chakra). Picture a band of white light moving in a circular motion between your heart and belly for a few moments. With practice, you'll start to feel the energy moving. Now move your left hand up to your throat (fifth chakra) and your right down to a spot below your belly button (second chakra). Expand the circular band of white light to now move from below your belly button, up to your throat, down through your heart and belly and back to the spot below your belly button, then up again. Do this for a few moments. Next, move your left hand up to the top of your head (your crown or seventh chakra) and move your right hand to a spot near where your legs meet your torso (the first chakra). Expand the circular band of energy to encompass all these chakras or energy points. Do this for a few moments. When you are done, place both your hands over your heart and say: "I am." This acknowledges the divine spark within you. You can balance yourself in the morning before you start your day or in the evening, especially if you've had a stressful day.

What Does it Mean to be an Empath?

Empath is the name given to an individual who is basically a human sponge, feeling everyone's emotions, whether it is through personal interactions or on a global scale. Many people consider this a curse, but it's a blessing when you consider that the job of an empath is to change the energy that they're feeling. Every thought, every emotion that a human being experiences goes out into the air. If a person had a bad life, what happens? That energy goes out. If they had a good life, that energy goes out as well. An empath who feels all that energy has two choices. They can medicate themselves so they don't feel anything anymore, or they can learn to deal with it through the process of grounding. Because this is something that is not talked about much, people who feel so much tend to "own it." In other words, they don't move the energy and it clings to them, weighing them down, especially if it's a frenetic or depressing energy. (Think about feeling everyone's emotions in a mall during the holiday season.) However, it doesn't matter if the emotions an empath is feeling are their own or someone else's. The idea is to ground out the energy to increase their own personal vibration. The more they increase their vibration, the more they increase their ability to love. And that love reverberates out. It's like a pebble thrown out into the water. It causes a ripple effect. As an empath, a person can change the energy around them by raising its vibration.

When it comes to dealing with spirits, it is important to remember that everything is energy, including our own. Each human being comes to this life to learn certain lessons. It's like climbing a stairway. Each lesson you learn, you go up a step. What happens if a person didn't live the life they were supposed to live? They don't reach that threshold that allows them to see the Door at the time of death. So what does that spirit do? They wander, looking for the energy that they feel most comfortable with. For example, if a person died an alcoholic, they're going to seek out the living who are alcoholics because that's the energy they're comfortable with. As a living person, if you feel a spirit around you, (and you will know if you suddenly find yourself feeling emotions that you weren't feeling a few moments before), you can go through those emotions for them. It needs repeating that ghosts no longer have a body to process those emotions, but we do. We open our hearts, change those old emotions they're still holding onto by moving the energy through us. It brings them up to that threshold and once they reach it, they can go through the Door. You can't destroy energy. You can only raise its vibration.

Centering Yourself

If you feel yourself losing control of your emotions and grounding isn't enough, try centering yourself by doing the following: Close your eyes and imagine the top of your head as the top of a triangle. Your left and right hands are the left and right sides of the triangle. The bottom of the triangle runs along your belly. Now focus on the top of the triangle. It may actually feel that it's not centered over the top of your head. If it isn't, gently push the top of the triangle until it's resting right above the crown of your head. Once you've gotten the top of the triangle centered over your head, imagine white light pouring into the top of the triangle, down into your body. What you are doing is establishing a connection back to Source. Now take all this white light and ground it out the bottom of your feet. You should start to feel yourself centered and balanced. Reconnect to Source during the day so you stay in the flow of energy.

Spirit Attachment and a Primer on Demons

We have found many instances where a living human has actually attracted a wandering soul to themselves because the two share a common denominator. This is known as a spirit attachment. It doesn't matter if the spirit is someone you've never heard of. What's attracting them to you may be something as simple as a shared experience. For example, a person who was an alcoholic in life will be attracted to that energy in death, because that is the energy they are most familiar with. In the Chapter 5 story, the spirit of the young girl was attracted to Cindy because she'd been in abusive relationships and that was the energy the girl knew.

As for demons, they are not as prevalent as is depicted on television. However, they do exist. The following is what we've discovered during our investigations regarding these darker entities.

Task-Maskers

This is a name that we gave to entities who appear to us as black-hooded figures. They will attach themselves to people who are going through a fearful, traumatic period in their lives. These are entities that are actually created by our own fears. We create them. They feed off our fears, amplify our fears, and try their best to keep us mired in dysfunctionality in order to continue to feed off that energy.

Lower-Energy Demons

The method we use to distinguish between whether a haunting is being caused by an angry spirit or a demon is that a lower-energy demon is one-dimensional. A spirit that was once human will retain human emotions. We will feel their anger, guilt, rage, etc. However, a demon doesn't have those emotions. They will attach themselves to a specific vulnerability of the living. Unlike Task-Maskers, these entities have been in existence since the beginning of time. In Randy's case, his vulnerability was the darker side of his personality that shunned human contact. He created barriers through drugs and alcohol to isolate himself from everyone. This made him a prime target for this particular demon who kept him in that state of apathy and used him to its own end. We have found it's extremely difficult to rid a person of this type of entity unless they make an effort to change. The problem is that the demon will stay away for only so long. Then, if the living person refuses to make the necessary changes to their lives, it will come right back. Unfortunately, until Randy seizes the reins and takes control, this demon will continue to exist around him.

Next Level of Demons

These are stronger demons who have their own agenda and use that agenda to interfere with a person's life path for their own ends. We all come to this Earth with our own life plan – those lessons we need to learn to continue our journey. These demons don't feed off a person's dysfunction so much as actually interfere with their lives. Turn on the television and look at the fear that is sold every day. That collective fear is generating a lot of energy. These demons are feeding the flames of that fear to keep people in a perpetual state of unease. We leak a lot of energy when we react to that fear and take it on ourselves. We also become afraid of taking steps that may actually improve our lives. Who does all this fear benefit? These demons and task-maskers do, however, serve an important purpose. They are there to teach us. We have choices. We can heal. We can turn away from fear and drama. There is a balance to everything. Darkness is simply an absence of light.

Of course not all hauntings have this dynamic taking place. Sometimes a haunting is just a haunting – like Cindy being haunted by the previous owner who didn't like her. Still, it's always beneficial to try and heal those areas of your life that hold you back from achieving true peace and fulfillment. Fear, and the creatures that feed on that fear, are your biggest enemies.

A Word About Spirit Guides

Whether you believe in the paranormal or not, everyone has spirit guides. Sometimes guides come in the form of animals. In shamanism, we call them our animal totems. If an animal appears to you three times in a short period of time, it's a safe bet that this is your animal totem. There are sites on the internet that will tell you what the animal represents. For example, wolf is about teaching. Turkey is about family. Eagle and hawk are about seeing the bigger picture. Squirrel signifies harvest – time to start gathering something into your life.

There are also spirit guides. Guides, whether animal or spiritual, come and go in your life depending on where you are on your life's path. Many people believe that deceased loved ones serve as guides. Sometimes they do. But – and this is very important – a guide cannot tell you what to do. They cannot interfere with your free will. They can guide and suggest and step in to save you in an emergency. But if you find yourself with a guide who is telling you what to do, when to do it, or if you find yourself with a psychic who is telling you the same thing, run the other way.

We humans are a stubborn lot. Sometimes we have to be hit over the head to learn a particular lesson. What we perceive as bad may not be bad in the long run. Sometimes we need to go through something tough in order to learn. Guides know that. They will step aside and allow you to go through something because they know you need to go through it. You can always talk to them and watch for signs that they are listening, whether it is a calmness that comes over you, or a slogan on a truck that suddenly makes sense. When I was going through a particularly bad patch in my life, I was walking through the streets of Boston thinking about my situation and how I could escape it. I thought about a particular co-worker who was making my life a living hell. I wondered what I could do to change it all. I happened to look up at that moment as a truck passed by and I saw on its side the words "Let it Go." I knew this was a gentle reminder from Guidance. I realized at that moment that I was making myself sick by worrying so much about a person whose actions I couldn't control. I did let it go and although she didn't change, I chose to change how I reacted to her. About two months later, I was able to leave that job, met Steve, and the rest, as they say, is history.

Cutting Cord Attachments

This happens quite often and can lead to illness, exhaustion, and loss of vitality, as witnessed by Judi. There are several types of cording; one of the most common is coming into contact with someone who literally drains you of your energy. I'm sure most of you reading these words have experienced this at one time or another. You meet someone, you speak for a few minutes, and when you turn away, you suddenly find yourself exhausted. Or you have a friend who constantly uses you as a sounding board for all their problems. They feel great after your talk; you feel like a wet dishrag. Guess what? They've corded into you and have taken your energy.

So someone has corded into you. What do you do?

The first thing you do is try and find a quiet space. State your intention (either silently or out loud) that you wish to remove any and all cords from anyone who doesn't serve you. The reason you state the intention in this manner is that you may not want to remove cords from your husband/wife or children. Next, rub your hands together. With your dominant hand, gently scan your abdomen area. When I do this, I will feel what appears to be a cold spot above the area where the cord is. You may feel a tingling in your hand. Just know that the energy will feel a little different. Sometimes when you're doing this, when you hit the area where the cord is, you may actually see a face, get a name or get a sense of the person who has corded into you. With your dominant hand, pull the cord out and picture white light closing up the area where the cord was attached.

Something to keep in mind with cording is that if you come back in contact with the person whose cord you removed and allow yourself to get sucked back into their drama, or you find yourself thinking and dwelling over them, the cord will instantly reconnect itself.

No one should be feeding off your energy. Everyone should be getting their energy from the Higher God Source.

Also, if people feed off the living while they are alive, there is a high probability they will continue to feed off the living when they die. This is called a spirit attachment and is addressed in another chapter.

Raising Your Vibration

Here is a quick way to raise your vibration. The human body has seven major chakras (or energy centers). The first is located at the base of the spine, the second below the belly button, the third above the belly button, the fourth in the heart area, the fifth in the throat, the sixth on your brow, and the seventh on the crown or top of your head. Starting with the first, imagine a ray of white light bathing each chakra (which is shaped like a round disk). Continue up each chakra until you reach the 7th, which is on the top of your head. You may feel tingling in each chakra as you cleanse it. However, there are five other chakras located above your head. Try to see five round disks above your head and infuse each one with radiant white light. As you're traveling up each of these chakras, you should feel yourself getting lighter and lighter. You may feel yourself tingling. That's good. That means your vibration is rising as you go up each chakra. Keep in mind, however, this is a quick and easy way to raise your vibration. In order to keep your vibration high, you need to heal any issues that may reside in any particular chakra.

Working with a Spirit

In several of these stories, you will have noticed that we take turns "working with a spirit." What this means is that at the time of the investigation, a spirit may not be ready at that point to go Home. Unless a spirit is deliberately interfering with the living, we don't force them to go Home. Just as they had free will in life, we respect their free will in death. However, we find that after we do our circles, the spirit will attach itself to us. They know they have an opportunity to leave the in-between place, which is neither of this World or the next. One of us will volunteer to continue to work with the spirit – feeling their emotions, counseling them, reassuring them that it's okay to continue their journey Home. What we do is show them that they have a choice. They can continue to stay in the darkness of the in-between place, or move to a place of love and peace. After we have worked through their emotions and traumas, many choose love and peace. Wouldn't you?

Look at Other Alternatives

For those of you who might be interested in investigating haunted places, or who have had experiences with the Other Side, keep in mind two things. A person doesn't need to have died in a location to haunt that location. In life they may have been attached to a place and in death they return to it. As you've seen in these stories, you also may be a haunted person yourself and you will attract spirits to yourself through no effort of your own. You may be sitting in your living room one evening, with no particular thought or emotion and suddenly you feel angry or agitated for no reason at all. There's a good possibility that a spirit has entered your energy field. Use the grounding and centering techniques I've outlined in the book to assist that spirit. They may not cross, but you can help lighten them up.

If you are exploring historical areas, remember that not everything is written in the historical record. There are many "skeletons in the closet." Just because you may feel something that wasn't written about doesn't mean it didn't happen. As in Chapter 11, the Old Manse, we can only go by what we felt. Of course, it's wonderful if we do find historical confirmation. But again, don't completely discount a discovery just because someone didn't feel it proper to write about a scandal or a potential scandal. There are always emotional facts that may not correspond with the written facts. If you are psychic or sensitive to energy, keep digging to get behind the known story. You'll never know what you might turn up.

What Keeps This Energy Going?

Drama in life equals drama in death. There are no truer words when it comes to paranormal investigations. Death does not stop the drama. In Chapter 12, Edward Ellis' life was certainly dramatic, starting with the Millerite movement, the near loss of his property, the beating of his wife, and the loss of their baby. The record producer's life was dramatic, as well as the woman who eventually went insane in the house. Which begs another question. What kept this energy going over the years? It was the drama of the living feeding into the drama of the dead. Energy cannot be destroyed, but it can be changed. The continual feeding of the energy of drama by the living created an ambiance where anyone who was even the least bit sensitive would be affected to the point where, like Leah, it was overpowering her own energy and she found herself getting caught up in the frenetic, unfocused, and heavy atmosphere around her. She and others before her fed into the initial dramatic energy, amplifying it and keeping it going like logs on a fire.

As in other investigations we've conducted over the years, we've noticed there are people like Leah who are drawn to a location, not because they like it, but because they're meant to change the energy in some way. Through our help, Leah was able to break the cycle of the dysfunctional energy and claim the space as hers. The trick for her, and others like her, will be to stay out of drama. Change your energy and the energy around you changes as well.